Bearing Fruit In Old Age

by Randolph L. Ewers
with Jack Michael

II

Scripture quotations in this book, unless otherwise noted, are from, "*The New King James Version. Copyright © 1979, 1980, 1982, Thomas Nelson Inc., Publishers.*"

Bearing Fruit In Old Age
ISBN 0-9629844-4-2

Copyright © 1995
by Randolph L. Ewers

Published by:
Randolph Ewers
Servant's Heart Ministry
P.O. Box 654
Mandeville, Manchester
Jamaica, West Indies

United States Address:
Servant's Heart Ministry
450 Depot Street #205
Romney, WV 26757

Printed in the United States of America. All rights reserved under International Copyright Law. Contents and/or cover may not be reproduced in whole or in part in any form without the express written consent of the publisher.

This Book is Dedicated to:
My Wife, Trudee,
My children, Randy and Susan,
Who loved me
Despite my failures!

VI

Introduction

Meet Randolph Ewers, missionary to the island nation of Jamaica.

71 years young, still going strong for the Lord, and expecting many more fruitful years of service for the kingdom of God!

Go back with me through the years and read about a 16 year old boy who; although he didn't know God; prayed that his mother might be healed.

Read about this same young boy who was called to the ministry at an early age, but chose rebellion instead of obedience to God.

Experience the Lord's hand of protection upon Randolph as an 18 year old Army Medic, serving his country on the battlefields of World War II; only to be sent home to spend the rest of his life in a mental institution.

Read about how God delivered him, and gave him his Army nurse for a wife.

Walk with Randolph through the family corporation's 2000 acres of land; which contained 1000 acres of apple, peach and cherry orchards; as he built his life on earthly wealth.

Be amazed as Randolph; one of the most prosperous men in his area; finally gives his life to Christ at the age of 53, and begins to discover his real purpose in life.

Follow Randolph through 10 years of lay ministry as he shares the good news of Jesus Christ in a small, rural, West Virginia church; and in the camps of migrant orchard workers.

Witness the grace of God as Randolph becomes critically ill and dies; but is miraculously given back his life!

Be astounded as you read about the loss of his prosperous orchards to a devastating flood!

Marvel as Randolph, at the age of 65, sells his home and possessions; and by faith, answers God's call to the mission field.

This is Randolph Ewers, missionary to Jamaica. He has no intention of retiring, and spending his remaining years playing bingo at the old folk's home! He's not interested in square dancing at the senior citizen's club; or taking sea cruises with the golden age fellowship from the church!

Instead, he's wading through the sea of humanity that characterizes Jamaica; taking the love of God to the poor and downtrodden of that nation.

This is Randolph Ewers, still bearing fruit in old age, serving God with all of his strength until the day he goes home to be with the Lord!

                      Jack Michael
              Jack Michael Outreach Ministries
              Winston-Salem, North Carolina

Bearing Fruit In Old Age

"Those who are planted in the house of the Lord shall flourish in the courts of our God. They shall still bear fruit in old age; they shall be fresh and flourishing, to declare that the Lord is upright..." (Psalm 92:13-15).

"When you hear the Lord's voice, be obedient, and you will be blessed! It doesn't matter how unqualified you think you are! It doesn't matter how old you are! Just obey the voice of the Lord, and he will use you mightily!"

Randolph Ewers
Servant's Heart Ministry

x

Chapter 1

Foundations

I'll never forget that warm, Spring day in May of 1935. I was 10 years old at the time; my brothers were 11 and 6.

We were playing under the shade of a large tree when I heard my cousin, Nancy say, *"Here comes the hearse!"* My father had just passed away at the young age of 48, leaving my mother to raise us three boys on her own.

The later years of my parent's marriage was quite unstable. I can still recall the arguments about another women. Yet, my mother remained loyal to my father, despite encouragement from her family to leave.

I never really knew my father; and sadly, I cannot remember ever receiving any love from him!

Yet, despite the lack of a loving, personal relationship with my father, and despite his early death, we were not a poor family. We didn't encounter the economic hardships experienced by many single parent families. We were, what I would call, an upper middle class family.

My mother's forefathers had come to this Eastern Panhandle area of West Virginia in the early 1700's, and were some of its original settlers. My father's family later moved up from Virginia in the middle 1850's.

I can still remember hearing stories about Indians raiding the early settlements. I recall one particular story about the Indians capturing a young girl. She returned to the settlement when she was older, but eventually went back to live with the Indians.

Despite having to endure early hardships, my forefathers emerged as prosperous land owners. They engaged in various aspects of agriculture, owned slaves, and helped establish banks in the area.

They fought on the side of the confederacy in the Civil War; several giving their lives for that cause. Even when the war ended, and they lost much of their wealth, they remained on the land and continued to prosper.

My grandfather on my father's side helped begin the apple growing industry in the area, and eventually became a very successful orchardist.

Both of my grandfathers were directors of the local bank; and at the time of their deaths, they were among the wealthiest citizens of the area.

Even my mother became a good business woman, despite having to raise three boys by herself. She acquired a farm, rented houses; and after my father's death, turned our own house into a Tourist Home. This proved to be very successful, because there were no hotels or motels in our area.

Consequently, we were always considered upper middle class. I cannot remember our family not having domestic help in the house. They almost always drove new cars; and in general, enjoyed a lifestyle far above the average citizen of that area.

We faithfully attended the same local Church as my forefathers before me had done.

This church was attended by most of the leaders, and the so-called prestigious people of our community, creating the impression that the church was a *"notch"* above other churches.

Yet, despite these high-minded attitudes of snobbery, as well as some old, dead, religious traditions, there was an inner core of people in the church who were truly devoted to God.

As for myself, I didn't know Jesus Christ as a young man. Without a father's influence and guidance, I grew up somewhat proud and rebellious. At age of 17, my mother, in act of desperation, shipped me off to military school.

Fortunately, God had his hand upon my life, even though I didn't realize it. His grace sustained me through years of pride, rebellion and disobedience; finally, and faithfully, bringing me to the purpose which he had ordained for my life!

Chapter 2

A 16 Year Old Experiences God

It was the middle of December during my junior year in high school; and our basketball team was playing one of its biggest rivals. I was looking forward to the game, and hoping to see my girl friend.

My mother had been sick for weeks and was not responding to treatment. Our family doctor; a close friend; was doing all he could. Nurses attended to her around the clock.

The nearest hospital was 35 miles away, which was a long distance back then. At this time in our history, you were mostly born, and died at home!

I was about ready to depart for the game when the doctor somberly emphasized that it would be best if I did not go. My mother had taken a turn for the worst!

My grandmother, and one of my aunts were at our house that evening. I overheard them talking about which relatives would take us boys once my mother died.

Panic struck me! I rushed out of the house, and began walking rapidly toward the edge of our small town of about 1,700 residents. It was very cold and the snow crackled under my feet. I eventually came to a field where we often played with our snow sleds. I fell on my knees and began crying out to a God that I really did not know!

I don't remember how long I was there. I just knew I needed help! The only one I knew to call upon was the God I was taught about in Sunday School.

I forgot about the cold. The night was crystal clear; it seemed that every star in the sky was visible. I could see my breath as I talked to God.

After praying, I scrambled to my feet, not knowing if my prayer had been heard. But, I did know that I had prayed in earnest, a prayer of desperation, a prayer with all my heart.

The doctor, my grandmother and my aunt were staying overnight. When I arrived back home, I inquired about Mom's condition. The answer, *"not much change!"* I went to bed expecting to hear the worst in the morning.

The next morning, I sprang from the bed my older brother and I shared, ran downstairs and hopefully inquired, *"how's Mom?"*

I was both surprised and overwhelmed by the answer. *"She's changed for the better,"* came the nurse's reply. God had answered my prayer! The doctor, my grandmother and my aunt had all gone home! I will never forget the emotion I felt at that moment!

In the following days, Mom continued to improve, and was fully recovered after about six weeks. I felt a great relief that my brothers and I were not separated and farmed out to live with different relatives. My mother lived to see all her children grown and married.

I really longed to tell everyone what had happened. How I had prayed, and how God had answered. I wanted to tell my mother first, and then everyone I knew.

Unfortunately, I didn't share this great victory. I was reared in an environment where you were expected to keep such things to yourself. Supposedly, such things were private matters between you and God alone.

Many years later, just a few years before my mother passed away, I finally shared this great blessing with her.

At this time; even though I didn't know Jesus Christ as my personal Lord and Savior; I was nonetheless very aware of the fact that God was doing something in my life!

At that time, even though I was only a 16 year old boy, I thought about going into the ministry!

Of course, I never mentioned it. Such a career path would not have been encouraged by my family. We were a very prosperous family, having acquired large parcels of land; and I was fully expected to follow in the family tradition as a fruit grower.

Neither was going to college encouraged, or considered to be necessary. Eventually, I would come into an inheritance, receiving a portion of my family's wealth!

Chapter 3

A Rebellious Boy

One of my best friends was a doctor's son. I couldn't help but notice that the family seemed to have everything materially.

Our family doctor; who was a close friend of my mother; had a summer cottage and was also very affluent.

When I went to summer camp, many of my friends there were doctor's sons, and the economic gap seemed to prevail.

I decided to become a doctor. I would serve God, serve mankind, and of course, become wealthy! I signed up for high school classes that hopefully would lead to medicine.

Much to the dismay of my family, I also decided that I wanted nothing to do with the land. That type of lifestyle was for those who were uneducated!

Of course, this dream of being a doctor was never realized. I was never at the top of my class academically. I was never chosen as a class officer; or received any of those prestigious high school awards. In fact, It seemed like everything I tried turned out mediocre.

I also desired very much to be athletic, but just couldn't seem to make the teams. I was asthmatic and would often develop severe chest colds and ear infections. Little did I know that there was an underlying cause that would one day almost take my life.

In frustration, I abandoned those lofty, unobtainable goals, and became friends with a wild group of kids who enjoyed the fast life. I became rebellious, and my mother completely lost control of me.

Every Saturday night, we went dancing, drinking, running around with the wrong type of girls, and getting into a lot of fights.

I was expelled from high school on three different occasions. It was only because of my family's influence that I was allowed to return to school after the third expulsion.

One day when I came home from school, there sat the high school principal, my uncle, who was a prosecuting attorney, the family doctor, and my mother. In exasperation, she had asked them to come talk to me.

The conclusion to the matter was; that I should be enrolled in a military school. It was thought that I would receive more discipline there.

Also, I was dating a girl that my family did not approve of, and it was thought that military school would end this relationship.

So, the following Fall, I was shipped off to military school. I soon discovered that many of the students there were from broken homes or had past experiences similar to mine.

It was my first time away from home, and I was very homesick. Nevertheless, I persevered through the year, and for the first time in my life, actually made some real progress.

At the end of the school year, I was given the achievement medal for the student who had made the most improvement that year. I was quite proud. It was the first recognition I had ever received!

During that school year, the United States entered World War II. I will never forget the day Pearl Harbor was bombed. I was only 17; but that event not only changed my life, but also the lives of an entire generation!

One might think that a year in military school would have changed my attitudes; but unfortunately, that old rebellion cropped up again! Without Jesus Christ in my life, military school was a temporary solution. What I needed was a permanent change in my heart!

After the summer break, I refused to go back to military school. I learned that my old girl friend was available. She had just broken off a relationship with the boy she was dating while I was away.

I reentered the local high school, and tried to rekindle the relationship with this old girl friend. I was shocked to discover that she was pregnant by her former boy friend.

Briefly, I tried to start a relationship with another girl, but she wasn't interested. So, I just became all the more rebellious!

The year was 1943, and I was 18 years old. World War II was raging, hot and heavy; and like almost all of my friends, I was on the verge of being drafted into the military!

Chapter 4

The War Years

It was July of 1943 when I received my draft notice. I was 18 years old. World War II was rapidly escalating.

Everyone's ears were alertly tuned to the radio. Much of Europe had fallen to Hitler's Nazi onslaught! Russia was on the verge of collapse! England was being bombed daily! Japan was swiftly moving to take all of Asia and the South Pacific!

I was sent to Texas for basic training; and subsequently selected for training as an Army Medic. We went through all the rigors of infantry training, but without rifles!

It's interesting how a type of camaraderie develops among military people, especially so during war years.

During my basic training, I became close friends with a boy who was a strong Catholic. Every Sunday, we would attend Mass together. I felt very close to God. I seriously considered becoming a Catholic. Later in the war, he suffered the trauma of being taken as a prisoner of war.

After he returned home and married, he named his son after me. I have never been more honored. When he died in 1990, I gave the eulogy at his funeral.

After basic training, I was sent to a camp in Indiana to be trained as a surgical technician. Finally, in June of 1944, I received my orders for overseas duty.

These war years produced so many unforgettable memories, some good and some bad. I'll never forget the huge waves as we traveled in a convoy of ships across the North Atlantic. You could look to the front and to the rear and see ships for miles!

We landed at Liverpool, England, and a few days later were transported by landing craft to Omaha Beach on the northwestern coast of France.

The grim evidence of a bitter conflict was all around us. The area was scarred with fresh evidence from recent fighting. The fury of the conflict could be charted by the debris which littered the beach.

There were breached shore defenses, burned and rusting tanks, and minefields still in the process of being cleared.

There were heaps of stone and lath where homes had once stood. Multiple shell craters; where blooming flower gardens were once prolific; stretched endlessly along our line of march.

But, the sight which caught and held my eye was a green field covered with row upon row of small, white crosses. There, still in formation, lay the soldiers who had unlocked the door to fortified Europe!

That first night, we stayed in fox holes and attempted to get some sleep. Our efforts were in vain as the beaches were continually bombarded throughout the night. The earth literally shook, and the sky was lit up by the blast of artillery shells.

That next morning, a third of our group was dead! We hadn't even seen any action!

The French town of Saint-Lo had just fallen to the Allied advance, and we were rapidly dispatched to replace medics who had been killed.

I felt certain the war would be over soon. German prisoners, six abreast, passed us on the road. The camp where they were being detained was jammed. I can still see these prisoners picking lice off their bodies.

We were trucked as close as possible to the front, then marched the rest of the way. The artillery fire became louder and louder!

We sat down for a brief rest; I turned, looked behind me, and saw a dead American soldier. I watched as a fly crawled into his mouth.

Night came and the skies were again lit up by parachute flares and the blast of bombs and artillery shells. By morning, I was in the thick of the battle. I was attached to Company D, 110th Infantry Regiment, 28th Division.

We had all been given a New Testament by the Gideons organization as we walked up the gang plank boarding the ship that transported us to England. I had not yet read any of it.

But, while in England, I began to think about how God had answered my prayer and healed my mother. The evening before I departed for France, I had attended a Protestant service held in an open field. I took communion, and to the best of my ability at that time, dedicated my life to Christ.

Now, here I was in the thick of the battle, and had no one to turn to but God! I prayed constantly!

Death was all around me. Bulldozers removed bodies from the roads so advancing troops could pass! To the best of my ability, I tried to help the wounded. Some were terribly mutilated!

I was wearing woolen OD's that were full of dried blood! If I could have stepped out of them, I believe they would have stood on their own!

In the evenings before dark, we searched the fields looking for the wounded. In that part of Northern France, the fields were all arranged in hedge rows. I remember finding a soldier clutching tightly to his New Testament. He was praying that someone would find him!

I kept repeating the first lines of Psalm 23, *"The Lord is my shepherd; I shall not want. He maketh me to lie down in green pastures: he leadeth me beside the still waters. He restoreth my soul..."* (KJV). That was all I knew, but those few words sustained me!

The Third Army was attempting to make a clean sweep of the area as we advanced toward Paris. Each day we kept moving forward. First, there would be heavy, and sometimes prolonged bombardment, and then, the infantry would inch forward.

The enemy would set up machine guns in the corners of a field and engage us in a cross fire. One morning as we were moving down the side of a hedge row, a line of bullets came right up the hedge, hitting several of the men. A bullet hit beside my right shoulder, another beside my left shoulder. It was evident that God had his hand upon my life!

A small group of soldiers to which I was attached advanced to the end of the field, but were cut off by Germans on the other side of the hedge. They kept throwing hand grenades and concussion grenades, killing or wounding everyone except me.

My best friend, another medic, was killed. I snatched his helmet, because somehow in the battle I had lost mine! In a daze, I wandered to the other side of the hedge and came face to face with the enemy. I quickly withdrew, and fortunately was able to link up with the rest of my company.

It's funny, but I held on to my friend's helmet all the way back to the states. It helped to save my life, and therefore became a very meaningful possession.

Later that day, after the infantry had completed their sweep through the area, I was scouting the field, looking for the wounded. I heard noises by a hedge row. To my great surprise, a German soldier walked out, dropped his rifle and cartridge belt, put his hands behind his neck, and yelled in the German language, *"I surrender!"*

The next thing I knew, another German soldier came out of the hedge row and did the same thing! I had taken two prisoners without firing a shot!

I'm sure they surrendered to me because of the red cross on my arm band and helmet. Realizing I was a medic, they probably thought they would be safe.

Had I been a regular infantry soldier and shot the first German, the second one almost certainly would have killed me!

For several hours, I used these captured prisoners as stretcher bearers, helping me to evacuate the wounded.

They showed me photographs of their wives and children relaxing on a Sunday afternoon. Prisoners always did this, so that hopefully, someone would have compassion on them! Their lives were of little value at this time.

The hatred was so intense. All too often, German prisoners did not live to see the POW compound. I've seen men step on a dead enemy soldier's face and twist their heel.

I'll have to admit, that hatred was in me too! It took me many years before I was able to talk to a person from Germany.

I even remember an incident within the past couple of years. I was invited to a dinner, and happened to be seated beside a Christian lady from Germany. I still had uncomfortable feelings inside of me!

But, praise God, I've been delivered from that hatred. God has forgiven me of so much. How can I help but forgive those who sought to harm my life!

The next day, another medic and I were on a small hill. Something told me to move! No sooner had we moved when a shell landed in that very spot! God had his hand upon me! He had other plans for my life!

One day we were huddled in fox holes; shells were falling all around. Suddenly, I heard this *"clop, clop, clop!"* I looked up and here comes a woman in wooden shoes. She was in a daze, her hair was in disarray; but she was carrying a rosary and praying.

I don't know about the rosary, but I know God answered her prayer and saved her life! This incident had a profound impression upon me. I realized that God hears and answers prayer, even in the midst of extreme danger!

And then, suddenly, my war was over! I don't remember everything. A tank was hit, and the man climbing out of the top was on fire. I could hear an incoming 88 as we were moving up a road. The man in front of me had his head blown off!

The next thing I remember, I was on a stretcher behind the lines. I had what is commonly called *"Shell Shock!"* I was completely disoriented, just as much a casualty of war as if I had taken a bullet in the stomach!

I was transferred to an Army hospital in Southhampton, England. I remember seeing rows of tents filled with wounded soldiers.

Despite my condition, I couldn't help but notice a certain young nurse who checked my papers. She was so friendly and full of life. I noticed that all the ambulatory patients were hanging around her. What an unusual place for happiness! I must meet this girl!

Before long she came by my litter. Her name was Trudee, and she had noticed that I was from West Virginia. I was happy to learn that she was from a small town near my home. Of course, I had no idea that she would one day become my wife!

One morning, she came by and gave me some advance notice. I was being moved, *"but don't tell anyone I told you,"* she emphasized! Eventually, she said, I was going home; and she asked that I visit her parents and tell them she was doing fine.

First, however, there was another ordeal that I had to endure! One from which only God could deliver me!

I was transferred to a mental hospital for treatment of what they called, battle fatigue. All around me were severe cases of mentally disturbed soldiers. Potentially, I was one of them!

I was placed in a locked ward, and given electric shock treatments! I was thrown into cold showers, and sometimes confined in a straight jacket. I banged my head against the padded walls and cried out for God to deliver me!

Then, one day, they told me I was going home! Things are still rather vague. I don't remember everything that transpired. I was on a rapidly moving train; the fields and trees were flying by. Then, I was on a ship. I was standing on the deck; a nurse was explaining to a blind soldier what the skyline looked like as we approached Charleston, South Carolina. I was home!

For years after the war, I was not able to be around gun fire, or even loud noises. Once at a fourth of July family picnic, a young man playfully threw a firecracker under my chair.

It threw me into such a state of confusion that I had to see a doctor. Even to this day, I will not go to a war movie, or watch one on television!

For a number of years, I carried a heavy burden of guilt, as if I had let down my fellow soldiers. I was not a war hero! My wounds were not like others who had been shot or killed! I didn't receive a Purple Heart metal!

Eventually, I came to the realization that I had no control over what happened. I was wounded psychologically; and was as much a casualty as any soldier on the front lines!

Several years after the war, I received a phone call from a Red Cross lady who served in France during the war. She had also visited me in the hospital in England. When I told her I was working, she couldn't believe it! She was certain that I would always be a patient in a psychiatric ward!

It took me about 50 years to recall all these events. I never wanted to talk about them; but God impressed upon me that I was to put them in this book!

I believe God wants to show that his hand of protection is upon those he has called! In me, he has shown forth his power to deliver, to heal, and to use someone that the world had given up as hopeless!

"For I know the plans I have for you, declares the Lord, plans to prosper you and not to harm you, plans to give you hope and a future." (Jeremiah 29:11 NIV).

Chapter 5

The Return Home

After returning to the states, I was hospitalized near Norfolk, Virginia. In the early part of 1945, I was released from the hospital and discharged from the military. By the spring of that year, the war in Europe was over, and Japan surrendered soon thereafter.

I came home as a deeply scarred, young man with no direction for my life. I found it difficult to settle down. I started drinking and carousing as before the war, only more so!

In those days, because of the GI bill, it seemed like almost every ex-soldier was going to college. I decided to do the same.

I had always wanted to go to college. Maybe I could realize my dream of becoming a doctor. So, two days before the beginning of the school year, I enrolled in the University of West Virginia.

I was advised by a doctor not to enroll in college. He said I was still too unstable. His diagnosis proved to be accurate.

Once again, I started running around with the wrong crowd. In my little group of college buddies, we were especially determined not to submit to anyone's authority. Rather than studying, we caroused the streets at night, looking for trouble, and frequently finding it!

One night, there was a severe fight. I was badly cut with a beer bottle. The police intervened and sent us back to our dormitories. The next day, I went home, never to return to the university.

It seemed like my entire life to this point had been a complete failure. In high school, I was never able to compete in sports. I was not an outstanding student. I had not held any class office. I was expelled three times.

The war years were no better. I had high hopes of attending officer's training, but had not succeeded. I went into the Army as a private, and came out as a private!

Now, I had also failed at the university! I just became all the more rebellious.

As I look back, I can clearly see God's hand upon my life; but at that time, I refused to yield my life to him.

In 1946, I announced to my mother that I was going to operate a small orchard which my brothers and I had inherited from our grandfather.

I definitely did not want to be an orchardist. I thought I could do better in some other endeavor, where there was more excitement. But, after my withdrawal from the university, this seemed to be the only option.

I threw myself into the work with all the determination I could muster. I would look at the big, old, oak trees on the property, and say, *"from little acorns, big oaks grow!"*

One day I was visiting our local hardware store; one of those stores that has everything. The owner was one of the most respected citizens of our community, and was known for his strong, Christian character.

He said to me, *"Randolph, I hear you're entering the business world. I would like to offer you a little advice."*

"In business," he explained, *"there are always up's and down's; and whenever you find yourself in the position of not being able to pay your creditors, go to them, explain your situation. Almost always, they will show you a little leniency until you're able to pay. On the other hand, if you run from your creditors, they won't have much understanding!"*

As I was leaving, he added, *"Randolph, don't forget to give 10% of your income to God!"* I didn't forget; and since becoming a Christian, I've always followed that advice!

Also, there have been quite a few times through the years that I've had to talk with my creditors. They have always shown leniency!

My future wife, Trudee came home from the war, and we started dating. This whole matter was sort of a surprise to her. She didn't think I would be around after the war to date her, or anyone else! She was certain I would always be in the mental hospital!

So, here I was, a former Army private, who had been discharged from a mental hospital; now courting a 2nd Lieutenant, who was my former nurse, and had seen me at my very worst. I guess it didn't look like I had very much to offer her!

Trudee moved up to Washington, D.C. to work for a pediatrician; and I began to make regular trips to visit her. Sometimes, she would visit her parents in nearby Cumberland, Maryland, and I would always arrange a date. We were engaged in 1947, and married a year later.

The Lord sure works in mysterious ways. I had to go all the way to England, and be hospitalized as a combat casualty in order to meet an Army nurse from a town next door!

Trudee and I have now been married for 46 years. We have two children, and three grandchildren.

Chapter 6

Beginning Seeds of Success

When Trudee and I were first married, we rented a small, farm house from my mother. In many ways, it was a good life. We had chickens that provided us with eggs, as well as meat. There were cows that provided us with milk, from which we churned our own butter. We raised a couple of pigs that we eventually butchered. And, we had a young calf, which eventually became our own cow.

But, these new beginnings also had their difficulties. At the time, Trudee was not able to drive; and being that she was from the city, this farm life was a big adjustment for her.

I was getting up at 5:00 AM, driving 12 miles to the orchard, and not returning home until around 6:00 PM; so we didn't see much of each other during those early years.

We started raising chickens to be used as broilers; and Trudee would sometimes spend hours just watching these chickens go about their daily routine. Not exactly a life of adventure for a former Army nurse who had experienced the horrors of World War II!

However, one day when I came home, she shared a fresh, new, combat story. She took me to the chicken house, and showed me two, huge rats she had killed with a rake handle. She first threw the cat into the feed barrel, where the rats were; but the rats were so big that the cat came out faster than he went in! Trudee was fortunate that the rats didn't scurry up the rake handle and bite her!

Yet, during this period of our lives, we spent as much time together as possible. Our little farm house bordered a river, and in the warm summer evenings, we would walk down to the river and catch a few fish.

After three years of renting the little, farm house, we managed to buy a home of our own. We paid $3,000.00 for it, which was a lot of money back then!

We badly wanted children, but we had a struggle in this area also. Every time Trudee got pregnant, it would end in a miscarriage.

One evening when I came home, she was in bed. A nurse was attending to her. She had been bleeding, so we rushed her to the hospital. The doctor informed us that she had not only lost a baby, but unfortunately, he also had to remove an ovary!

The doctor said he should have removed both ovaries, but because Trudee wanted to have children so badly, he left the other one. But, then he added, that although leaving her with one ovary might give her hope, it was his professional opinion that we would never have children. We were both heart broken.

After about three more years, due to the fact that our business was beginning to prosper, we moved to one of the larger houses on the orchard.

My brothers and I began to buy additional orchards for some very reasonable prices; and due to inflation, their value rapidly increased.

Then, we would borrow money on our existing properties, and purchase even more orchards. We figured that if we kept investing in land, when we finally sold out, we would all have a comfortable retirement.

During this time, there was a large migration of people into our county from Baltimore, Maryland and Washington, D.C. The land was cheap, and people were buying up all the available farms for weekend retreats, summer vacation homes or investments for the future.

A millionaire from the Washington, D.C. area was one of those buying up tracts of land. We sold him a few of our farms for an excellent price; and then reinvested the money into two of the choicest orchard properties in the Romney, West Virginia area.

The land totaled over 1,200 acres, and there were existing orchards on about 600 of these acres. Finally, from little acorns, big oaks had grown. We had become one of the biggest fruit growers in the state of West Virginia, and the surrounding area.

On a good year, our orchards were producing 200,000 bushels of apples, 20,000 bushels of peaches, and 20 tons of cherries.

In time, we bought the local, cold storage cooperative, which provided us with ample facilities for storage and packing.

Now, since we were able to store apples the year round, we got into the gift packaging business, and began shipping fruit from one season to the next.

We were employing about 50 people year round, and during the harvest seasons, our payroll jumped up to around 150 people.

It was during this time, that we began to utilize a program which allowed us to bring in foreign workers; and this is how I first became involved with the Jamaican people.

Looking back, it sure is interesting how God works out his plans for our lives. At that time, I didn't have a clue as to what God was doing!

Chapter 7

A Heritage from the Lord

"Behold, children are a heritage from the Lord, the fruit of the womb is His reward." (Psalm 127:3).

Trudee and I were determined to have children. If she couldn't have children naturally, we would consider other means! We began to explore the possibilities of adoption.

It was difficult to adopt a child in our area. As is frequently the case, there weren't enough babies available to meet the demands of those desiring to adopt.

One day, the doctor called us; the same doctor who had attended to Trudee during her last miscarriage.

He informed us of a baby that was available for adoption. A certain young girl from a prestigious family had gotten involved with a married business man. Both were from good backgrounds, and the families wanted to keep the matter confidential.

Finally, the day arrived when we were to receive this baby; but once again, we were disappointed. At the last minute, the child care center stepped in and put a stop to the adoption. They said we could not adopt this particular child because we were residents of another state.

Obviously, this was big blow, but we refused to give up! We applied to the state of West Virginia for adoption.

It was six months later when we received a phone call that a baby boy from the Welch, West Virginia area was available for adoption.

We left early one morning for the long trip to the little town of Welch; a mountainous area located in the southern part of West Virginia, just north of the Virginia border.

This was my first trip to this part of West Virginia. We were from the eastern Panhandle area, which was a very prosperous agricultural region.

I was shocked by the unemployment and the poverty! At one time, when coal was king, this had been an affluent county.

However, due to a sharp decline in the coal industry, unemployment was rampant. To this day, the economy in that area has not made a full recovery.

We trudged up a dirty set of stairs to the adoption center, which oddly enough, was over the Greyhound Bus Station.

When we first saw this baby boy, we were disappointed. He was one year old. We were expecting a new baby; two, maybe three weeks old. The case worker encouraged us to stay for a while. Maybe we would get to know the baby a little better and change our minds.

Of course, she knew exactly what she was doing. In a very short time, this baby boy had won our hearts. Soon, we were gathering up his few belongings, ready to return home with a child of our own.

One of the toys he had was a spinning top. His foster parents had given it to him that very day as a present for his first birthday.

That night, we checked into a local hotel; and I went shopping for baby food. When I returned, my wife was crying. She showed me an unusual letter from the foster mother explaining how much they loved this little boy. They had wanted to adopt him, but the welfare agency said they were too old.

The letter contained the baby's name and background, and requested that we please stay in touch with them. All this was written in ink on the inside back of his undershirt, so the adoption agency would not find it!

We named our new baby boy, Randolph, after me, of course; and we loved him like he was our own natural child.

I can still remember the night he came to accept us. Trudee was preparing him for bed, and we were saying our prayers. As we ended our prayers, he jumped up and threw his arms around Trudee. At that time, he truly became our little boy.

And then, the God of miracles showed up! The following year, Trudee announced that she was pregnant!

We had been explicitly told that she could never have children. In fact, we had stated as much on the adoption application.

The doctor couldn't believe it; neither could he explain it! Surely, we serve a God of miracles! Sometimes, he has plans for us that we don't even know about.

Our daughter arrived early in the Spring. She was a healthy, beautiful baby; and Trudee had delivered her without any complications.

We named her Susan, after my mother. Now, we had a complete family!

Chapter 8

The False Pursuit of Happiness

When our children became old enough, we enrolled them in a Sunday School class. Every Sunday, we would drive 12 miles into Romney, and drop them off at the church. Then, we would visit with friends, and come back after Sunday School to pick them up.

I don't know why, but one day I declared that we would no longer leave them at Sunday School, but we would start attending also.

We not only started attending church; we became quite active in the church! Before long, I was teaching a Sunday School class; and in time, I became the superintendent.

Unfortunately, I remember several rude instances about this particular church. There was the time when we attended a Sunday School picnic. Everyone was supposed to bring food, and spread it out like a big *"Pot Luck."* However, when we arrived, we sat alone, and everyone else sat together and shared their food! Most of these people were my friends, I thought! Some were even my relatives!

I also remember a man who was given the option of attending church, or returning to jail. I guess you could say the justice system was little different in those days! Anyway, when he came to the church, nobody would accept him. I did my best to befriend him and be sociable; but when his time was up, he left the church and never returned.

One would think that such things would have discouraged us from continuing with the church, but for some reason, we didn't let them hinder us.

As I've said before, God had his hand upon me; and years later, we actually found a small core of people in the church who were sincerely desiring and seeking after the things of God!

We always had a wonderful place for our children to grow up. I had a riding horse, and the children had a pony. From our mare, we would sire and raise colts; and I would teach them to pull a sleigh during the Winter, and a buggy in the Summer.

Our home was always open to visitors, and we had frequent overnight guests. There were many family gatherings on both sides of the family. Homemade ice cream was a must, and the children would always help me crank the ice cream maker.

From an outsider's viewpoint, I was a solid citizen in the community. I belonged to the Masonic Lodge, 32nd. degree Mason, Eastern Star. I also belonged to the Shriners.

I was very active in horticulture societies and fruit related organizations, and helped to start a Ruritan in our area.

To some, It even appeared that I had a relationship with God. Strangely enough, I had become an elder in the church!

On the inside, however, I was empty! I didn't truly know God. I had not accepted Jesus Christ as my personal Savior. I did not have a born again relationship with God.

I kept very busy working in the orchards. In fact, you could say I was a *"workaholic!"* Money was the answer! If you had money, you had power!

I would say to friends at New Year's Eve parties, *"I wish you a prosperous new year,"* and then I would add, *"if business is good, you'll be happy, and if not, the year isn't worth celebrating!"*

But, the truth was, if a person couldn't *"scratch my back,"* professionally speaking, I didn't want them as friends, and I didn't have time for them!

I was careful to make friends with politicians who could assist me with acquiring a labor force for my orchards; or perhaps help open some other business door of opportunity. I could telephone our Senator, and he would talk to me!

I treated my employees well, but definitely did not consider them my equal. It was good to be friendly and show concern at work; but afterwards, I spent my time with so-called successful people, who I thought could help me make more money.

I loved to go to parties, and dance and drink. Trudee was more reserved, and went only because I insisted. Several times a year, I would also throw a large party at our home.

Sometimes, I would start drinking, and afterwards, could not account for my actions.

Yet, God always seemed to intervene in my life, whether I wanted him to or not! One evening when we had some friends over, I was pouring myself a drink of whiskey. I felt a tug on my pants, and looked down to see my son.

"Daddy," he asked, *"what are you drinking?"* I told him it was water, but he wasn't fooled. He said, *"that's whiskey!"*

That very moment, I decided that I would never drink again. I poured the whiskey down the sink, and have not had a drink since!

As our children grew into their adolescent years, they were both attractive, and had no trouble making friends, both male and female. Our home was always full of young people.

But, I regret not living a more spiritual life before my children. I regret not being more of a disciplinarian in dealing with them. Had I more closely observed scriptural principles of child rearing, I'm certain my children would have grown up differently.

The day came when, due to the buying and selling of various pieces of property; and due to a successful investment in the stock market; that we built a large, new home.

This new home was ninety feet long, and had a large veranda on the front overlooking the mountains. We filled it with valuable antiques, paintings, the very best in crystal and china, and we had enough place settings of sterling silver to seat 36 guests.

There was a swimming pool in the back with an enclosed porch overlooking the pool. The yard was an acre of landscaped flower gardens, and shaded, sitting areas. There was a 300 foot wrought iron fence in the front, with a large, wrought iron gate.

During the winters, there was a hill upon which to ride sleds; and a pond upon which to ice skate. In the summers, There were fields for horse back riding.

We had arrived, or so I thought!

Unfortunately, the happiness which I was pursuing continued to elude me. I discovered that happiness could not be attained through a large, fancy home.

I also discovered that happiness could not be attained through success in business; nor in the accumulation of money!

I decided that a divorce would provide me with the happiness I was seeking. I went to my cousin, who was a lawyer. I told him I wanted out of the marriage. I told him to give my wife anything she wanted. What Trudee wanted, was no part of a divorce!

I want to stop here for a moment, and give honor to my wife. I greatly appreciate her love and devotion through the years. The best day's work I ever did was to walk down the aisle and marry Trudee.

It was her supplemental income that enabled us to own our first home.

It was her love and discipline that played the larger role in the rearing of Randy and Susan. Most of the time, I was too busy with work, or too involved with my own problems to bother with them.

Probably no other woman in the world would have put up with my arrogance, pride and self-centeredness!

Of course, the divorce never took place. A fact for which I thank God!

Unfortunately, I made some other foolish mistakes in my fruitless search for happiness. One of the most painful involved an attempt to blackmail me for $5,000.00 with a cassette tape, that had been secretly made, which contained an immoral conversation!

It was 2:00 AM when I called two of my closest friends, a lawyer and a minister. They asked if I had any idea what time of the day I was calling? I said, *"yes, but if my life means anything at all to you, please come!"*

In tears, I confessed my sin. My minister friend read Psalm 51, a portion of which says, *"Have mercy upon me, O God, according to Your lovingkindness; according to the multitude of Your tender mercies, blot out my transgressions. Wash me thoroughly from my iniquity, and cleanse me from my sin....Purge me with hyssop, and I shall be clean; wash me, and I shall be whiter than snow."* (verses 1, 2 & 7).

I will never forget Trudee's response as we sat there on the sofa. She said she loved me, and forgave me! Those were the words I desperately needed to hear, for I was seriously considering suicide!

Unfortunately, There were other times when I foolishly considered suicide as the solution to my problems. One time, while we were living in the little, farm house, I sat with a rifle across my lap, and a yard stick to reach down and push the trigger. I spent the whole night, expecting to be dead the very next moment!

Deep down in my heart, I knew that total surrender to Jesus Christ was the answer to my problems; but for such a long time, I was too stubborn to make that choice.

But, thanks be to God, he always had his hand upon me! He kept me through all those difficult times when Satan was striving to steal my very soul!

Chapter 9

I Yielded My Life to God

There was a lady in our church who had heard of a Christian organization known as the Lay Renewal Group. Reportedly, this group; which was led by a medical doctor and his wife; had been used mightily by the Lord to bring spiritual revival to churches.

Our minister and certain other members of our church, myself included, felt that we needed a spiritual revival. I was soon to learn what an understatement that was!

We made contact with this doctor and his wife, and scheduled a four day, weekend, Lay Renewal Retreat.

I was asked to help establish a 24 hour period of intercessory prayer at the church. Members came in at different hours of the day and night to pray.

When the Lay Renewal team arrived, 12-15 in number, we opened up our home. We ended up keeping the leader and his wife. I had never seen so many people that seemed so happy!

Before the first service, the Lay Renewal team went into a private room at the church to pray. I was also invited. I never heard such praying in all my life! I felt the very presence of God! I told my wife later, *"I don't know what kind of prayer that group was having, but I know one thing; God was in their midst!"*

I was drawn to this Lay Renewal Group. I simply could not get enough of the word they were speaking. I knew they had something I didn't have; and I was going to search for it until I found it! Even after they finished at our church, I followed them around, attending their Bible studies and meetings!

After each service, the Lay Renewal would have an altar call. This was unusual because the church I belonged to didn't have altar calls. Regardless, during that weekend, they had altar calls anyway; always with the opportunity for people to accept Jesus Christ.

On the last evening, the church was full, approximately 300 people. We were sitting in the rear of the church. I told my wife, *"I'm going forward! I've tried everything else!"*

So, suddenly, here I was; a proud man; a leader in the fruit industry; an elder in the church; now kneeling in the altars and making a public profession of faith in front of all these people who knew me!

I felt someone kneel beside me. It was my wife. Together, Trudee and I gave our lives to Jesus Christ that night!

These meetings had a dramatic effect on our church. About 50 people went forward during that altar call! Prayer groups and Bible studies were formed; and the church became more open to the leading of the Holy Spirit. Today, the flame of revival still burns in that church!

It was March 20, 1977. I was 53 years old at the time, and I went *"hook, line and sinker"* for the Lord. It had taken what some would consider a lifetime for me to yield my life to God! I'm thankful for his mercy and patience toward me!

From that day, I could not get enough of the word. I read my Bible continually, rising at 5:00 AM to have two full hours with the Lord before going to work.

We opened our home to Christians from all walks of life. It was a joy to hear story after story about people who had been radically changed by the power of God.

I had heard of such people, but heretofore, I considered them as somewhat weird! Now, I was searching them out, and desiring to become their friends.

I attended prayer groups where believers were praying for healings, and taking authority over demonic spirits. This was all so new to me, but it was exciting! I was in so-called, *"seventh heaven!"*

Some of my new, Christian friends had been changed much more radically than I. The sins of their former life would have made them totally unacceptable in society; but they had been washed clean by the blood of Jesus; and now, they were discovering, and sharing the love they had never before experienced.

I remember one man who was a *"pimp"* in a *"red light"* district known as *"The Block"* in Baltimore, Maryland. I had visited this area once before I was a Christian. I have never seen so much filth, and open sex in my life!

When this man accepted Jesus Christ, he ran up and down *"The Block"* with his small son in his arms, crying, *"I am free! I am free at last!"*

Since then, I've met Christians who were formerly prostitutes, homosexuals, alcoholics, drug addicts, and criminals. They all expressed the same reaction, *"I am free! I am free at last!"*

And, that has been my song of deliverance! Jesus once said about a sinful woman who had washed his feet with fragrant oil, *"Therefore I say to you, her sins, which are many, are forgiven, for she loved much. But to whom little is forgiven, the same loves little."* (Luke 7:47).

Chapter 10

Sharing the Good News

    I had never been able to speak in public. It was difficult for me to say even a simple prayer! Had I ever been called upon to give the benediction at church, I probably would have run out the back door!
    Speaking or praying in public was only for those certain elders who had a deep commitment to God; or for the minister, who was not only educated, but paid for that purpose!
    In my line of work, I often received invitations to address different horticultural groups, but I refused because of a lack of confidence in my speaking ability.

Now, after receiving Jesus Christ as my Savior, I was willing and available to share this message of salvation to anyone and everyone who would listen!

My first opportunity to witness came in the fall of the year. I was invited to be a part of the same Lay Renewal Group that had been at our church.

Unfortunately, it was also harvest time. I would never leave my work during this time, regardless of the reason. This was what I had worked for the entire year; pruning, fertilizing, spraying, and nurturing the fruit until it was ready for harvesting.

Besides, our corporation; as was normal from season to season; had signed liens, and we were responsible for repaying the banks around one million dollars from the harvest.

I really wanted to go with the Lay Renewal Team, but there was just no way I could leave at this time!

I continued to ponder the invitation; but I was convinced that I just could not leave my work at this time of the year. It's crucial that you use every available hour during harvest time. If the fruit is not harvested at just the right time, it will drop off on the ground!

Yet, the Lord kept impressing upon me to go! Finally, I wrote a letter and accepted the invitation!

The day that Trudee and I were to leave, it was raining. This further complicated things, because rain stops the harvest!

The Lay Renewal weekend was scheduled from Thursday through Sunday. I decided that I couldn't go. If the rain stopped, we would have to work overtime, maybe even on Sunday, to make up for lost harvesting time.

Yet, the Lord kept firmly impressing upon me that I should go!

Finally, I told my secretary I was leaving. She informed me that we were short of the funds needed for payroll. During the harvest, our payroll was about $25,000.00 per week.

About that time, the field foreman came in and informed me that several tractors had broken down, and it was impossible to load the fruit and get it to the storage until they were fixed!

Within a few minutes, my cold storage manager showed up and informed me that several of the fork lifts had broken down, and he was unable to unload the trailers and put the apples into storage.

During this time, we were picking 5,000 bushels of apples per day. If the machinery did not get back into operation, there would be 10,000 bushels in the field the next day, and 15,000 the day after that!

Seemingly, it was absolutely impossible for me to leave! Yet, the Lord kept saying go!

I received a phone call. One of the trucks that was delivering a load of packed fruit was involved in an accident! The driver had been taken to the hospital, and the police had not yet determined who was at fault!

Obviously, it was not meant for me to go! I didn't realize it was the devil putting roadblocks in my way.

All of a sudden, I jumped up from my chair! I announced to my secretary that I was leaving immediately for a Lay Renewal weekend. *"Furthermore,"* I told her, *"I won't be back until Monday morning!"*

She said, *"what about the payroll?"*

I replied, *"people who have outstanding balances for previously shipped fruit will be sending in checks to cover the payroll; and furthermore, everything else will be all right as well!"*

She questioned my reply; or perhaps it was my sanity she was questioning!

As I left the office, many of the workers were waiting for their pay. They weren't concerned about the fruit. Since it was raining, they were just thinking about getting paid, and having a long weekend off from work.

One of them asked where I was going? I said, *"to witness for the Lord!"* They were all dumbfounded. They had never heard me say anything like this before!

The Lord used me mightily that weekend. The first evening service, I was asked to come forward and share my testimony. I had no reservations or nervousness about me at all. In fact, I couldn't hardly wait to share what God had done in my life!

From that time until now, I've been able to speak in public without fear. I've shared with a few; spoken to 2,000; and appeared many times on Christian television. The power of the Holy Spirit has changed my life!

Before I knew it, the weekend was over. I had seen many come forward to accept Jesus, and I was on fire for God!

Sunday afternoon, as we were nearing home, my wife asked if I was going to check with the different foremen to see how things had progressed at the orchards?

I told her, *"don't worry, it will all be there waiting for me in the morning."* As we drove along side one of the orchards, I couldn't help but notice that the fruit had been picked!

The next morning when I arrived at work, I was greeted by the cold storage manager. He said they had gotten the fork lifts repaired, and all the fruit was in the storage!

A foreman from the orchards informed me that the tractors had been repaired, and all the fruit had been hauled in! They were able to work late on Saturday, and the harvesting was up to date!

Next, the secretary informed me that a check had come in which covered the payroll; and we had money left over!

Finally, the truck driver who had been in the accident came in and informed me that he was not seriously hurt. The police were not holding him responsible for the accident; and the insurance would cover the damages!

I learned a valuable lesson that weekend, one that I have never forgotten. *"If you will do the Lord's word, he will look after your work!"* From that time, I have never allowed my business or personal life to keep me from serving God.

God began to use me everywhere. I was asked to share my testimony at a tent meeting. As I walked up the grass aisle and took my seat on the platform, I looked out over the large crowd, and remembered, *"these are the very people I used to make fun of!"*

When I was a young boy, My friends and I would sit on a hill, and laugh as these people began to shout and sing, and jump around.

Once, I went to a Oral Roberts healing service. I refused to believe that anything was happening. It was all emotion. These types of meetings were for poor, uneducated people!

I hung my head in shame. I now understood that these people had discovered something the world did not have. They were more blessed than all my worldly friends!

I thought about the time in Washington, D.C. when I attended a Billy Graham crusade. I felt the power of the Holy Spirit! I felt God calling me! I turned to a friend who was with me, and said, *"let's get out of here before I go forward!"*

I had suffered much before finally yielding my life to God; but it was all behind me now.

I had become a part of God's kingdom, and I was experiencing that which the Bible calls, *"joy unspeakable!"*

I've lost count of the churches where I've shared my testimony; but there are certain instances that *"stand out"* in my remembrance.

Once, I was with a Lay Renewal Team in Charleston, the state capitol of West Virginia. We were ministering in one of the most prestigious churches in the city.

I was asked to speak at a breakfast meeting at a fashionable restaurant atop one of the tall buildings. I walked in, carrying my Bible. People were lined up at the buffet table, talking, laughing and enjoying themselves; but as they noticed me, a hush seemed to fall over the place!

I was shown to a large table that was set up for the purpose of my visit. Seated at the table were executives from a local chemical plant as well as other area business leaders.

I placed my Bible on the table beside my plate. Everyone seemed very reserved and quiet. It was difficult to start a conservation!

Then, the Lord spoke to me, and said, *"take your Bible off the table!"*

I thought, *"Isn't that the purpose of my coming; to witness? Why remove my Bible?"* But, I was obedient. I placed my Bible under my chair.

Conversation started to flow, and before long, we were engaged in small talk. I guess they were intimidated by God's word!

When I was introduced, I started talking about the Lord. It was an informal setting, so whenever I would share with them about God, or Jesus, they would change the subject.

The Lord spoke to me again. *"Tell them about your business, and they will listen!"*

So, I told them about our 2,000 acres of land and orchards; and about the hundreds of thousands of bushels of fruit we harvested every year. I told them we grossed more than a million dollars each year; and they listened!

When they found out I was from the panhandle area of West Virginia, they started talking about deer hunting in that area. Some of them owned hunting lodges. Others knew the location of our orchards.

Gradually, I began to share how Jesus Christ had come into my life; and how he had taken care of my business, while I was taking care of his!

When the meeting was finished, they all shook my hand, and indicated that they would come to the Lay Renewal services.

That same night, one of those men came forward to receive Jesus. He and his wife had been separated, but during that service, they were reunited by the power of God!

I thank God for his wisdom, guidance and direction! He is God! I'm just his servant!

Chapter 11

Healed, and Filled with God's Spirit

During my childhood, I was asthmatic, and often suffered from severe chest colds. Several times the doctor was called to our home late at night, because I was unable to breathe.

Ten years before accepting Christ, I was very sick with blood poisoning, almost losing my life. I was at home in bed for a week before the doctor admitted me to the hospital. It turned out to be a one month stay.

Late one night, the doctor came by to check on me. He opened my eyelids, and was examining me with a small flashlight.

I got the distinct impression that the doctor thought I was going to die. I said to myself, *"like Hell I'm going to die!"* Soon, I got better, and was sent home to recuperate.

I didn't know it at the time, but in a crude sort of way, I was applying the scriptural principle of rebuking the devil. I was determined that I was not going to die!

There were other times that my life was spared from attacks of pneumonia and other potential disasters. There's no question that God had his hand upon me. He had work for me to do; and he wanted me to yield my life to him!

One year after accepting Christ, I started getting very tired, to the extent that I couldn't complete a day's work. This was unusual for me, because I was always on the move.

I started coughing up blood. It would stop for a while, then start up again. I went to a specialist, who used a bronchial scope on me, but couldn't find anything wrong.

For a while, the condition improved; but a few days before the 4th. of July, Trudee and I were attending a barbecue picnic at a friend's home. As I was walking by myself in the yard, I coughed up a large amount of blood. We had to leave early, as I was feeling really bad.

The next morning, the doctor admitted me to the hospital. He did another bronchial scope on me, but still found nothing wrong!

That evening, the doctor requested to do exploratory surgery on me; emphasizing that about 95% of the time, the symptoms I was exhibiting meant lung cancer! *"The quicker the cause was removed,"* he said, *"the better the chance of survival!"*

I lay there and thought to myself, *"the peach harvest is upon us, and after that, the apple harvest. A labor force has to be hired, and there are numerous other preparations that must be made before harvest."*

I asked if we could postpone the operation until after harvest? The doctor sensed an urgency that he should operate immediately!

I looked at him, and asked if he were a Christian?

He said, *"every morning before going on duty, I go to the hospital chapel, and pray for God's guidance!"*

I said, *"do the operation!"*

They prepared me that very evening for the operation. A Christian brother from our Bible study came and spent the night with me. I will always be grateful for his care and concern!

At 7:00 AM, they wheeled me into the operating room for what was supposed to be a three hour operation. Instead, the operation lasted until 5:00 PM that evening, a total of 10 hours!

After a short time in the recovery room, they took me to intensive care. My memory is vague, but I knew I was in very bad condition!

About all I can recall is someone putting ice on my lips, and in my mouth. That was a great relief! Four days later, they moved me to a private room.

There was no lung cancer. Instead, I had an extremely rare condition. At that time, only seven such cases had been reported to the American Medical Association. I can't even pronounce the medical terminology.

Basically, the two lower lobes of my right lung had calcified. This was caused by a birth defect; an opening in my esophagus, which allowed small particles of food to enter my bronchial tubes and get into my lungs.

I was told that this condition occurs in only one out of 34,000 births. Today, such conditions are discovered and corrected when a baby is born at the hospital.

However, I was born at home! So, this problem had been going on for the entire 54 years of my life. I'm sure this was the main reason why I wasn't very active as a child, and was never the achiever I longed to be!

This condition normally takes the life of those who have it, usually in their early years. Their death certificate would likely state that they died of pneumonia or blood poisoning.

It seemed like there was tube in every opening of my body. I knew I was very sick; and I was in much pain. Full recovery, if I recovered at all, was going to take a long time!

One evening, I told Trudee that the pain was leaving my body. She had an alarmed look on her face, and asked me to repeat what I had just said. I repeated once more that all the pain was leaving my body.

She hurriedly left the room, and within a few minutes, returned with the doctor and a team of nurses. I didn't know it at the time, but I was told later that when the pain begins to leave your body, it's a sign of impending death!

As the doctor and nurses were frantically working on me, something unexplainable and supernatural began to happen! I literally felt my spirit leave my body! Scientifically speaking, I suppose I was dead!

As my spirit hovered above them, I could look below and see the doctor and the nurses coming and going, very busily working on my body. It was like I was suspended in space!

Then, very distinctly, I heard the voice of my Heavenly Father. He said, *"because of the many prayers of intercession, I'm going to give you back your life; but, you are to serve me for the rest of your life!"*

My spirit immediately returned into my body. I felt the doctor slapping my face, and I heard him say, *"we almost lost you!"*

The time was 11:00 at night, but all this had started at 5:00 that evening. Trudee had time to call my family, and our minister; and they had driven 30 miles to be with her at my death!

The next morning, the doctor informed me I had a staff infection. They would have to reopen the incision where the lobes had been removed to allow the infection to come out!

The doctor explained that this procedure was potentially very contagious. Therefore, this follow-up operation was to be done right in my hospital room.

Furthermore, he explained, there could be no anesthetics, because the infection was all around my heart and lungs. He promised to be as gentle as possible, and stop when the pain became unbearable!

I thought to myself, *"this is like having a leg amputated without anesthetics!"*

I cried out to God for help. I didn't know much scripture at the time, but the Holy Spirit immediately brought this verse to my remembrance, *"If you abide in Me, and My words abide in you, you will ask what you desire, and it shall be done for you."* (John 15:7).

I prayed, *"God, give me the strength to be a good witness; that I would not cry out in pain!"*

A makeshift operating room, complete with operating table and lights, was set up in my room. The doctor and the nurses came in wearing masks and gowns. They lifted me onto the table and rolled me on my side.

I felt the stitches being removed, and felt the infection coming out of the opening and running down my back. It felt like a basin of warm water was being poured down my back!

Within a half hour, it was over. I had felt no pain whatsoever!

The doctor commented, *"you were a very good patient, Randolph. You never said a word. All you were doing was singing some unintelligible words!"*

I had no idea what he was talking about; and I definitely cannot sing! However, I do know that by God's grace, I had been carried into another realm, and had experienced no pain! I give all the praise to God!

After the operation, one of the attending nurses; who was a Christian; came in and explained the situation. *"The opening in your chest cavity was so big, I could stick my fist in it; and I could see your backbone!"*

And then she added, *"Mr Ewers, did you realize that you were singing and speaking in tongues?"*

Since that day, I have never ceased from speaking in tongues. Previous to this time, I knew absolutely nothing about speaking in tongues. I had never gone to a church where believers spoke in tongues, nor had I ever heard anyone speak in tongues!

No one can convince me that speaking in tongues is from the devil. It's a God given gift to be used in your prayer life; enabling you to have a more complete union with God.

God had given me this gift so that I could enjoy that more complete union; and subsequently, go forth with boldness to proclaim his mighty power!

As I reflect upon all these things:

(1) The fact that my operation was only the seventh of its kind reported to the American Medical Association.

(2) The fact that I could have died from blood poisoning or pneumonia, and the condition never found!

(3) The fact that such a complicated operation was successful!

(4) The fact that I died, and that my life was given back to me!

(5) The fact that God sovereignly filled me with his Holy Spirit!

(6) The fact that my Heavenly Father gave me a direct command to serve him!

How can I do anything less than be totally committed and obedient to God's voice!

Chapter 12

The Labor Camp Ministry

During the harvest season, we operated two labor camps. We brought in fifty workers from Jamaica, and another fifty from Mexico.

I would say our labor camps were above average. The buildings were constructed out of concrete, with different size rooms. Some of the rooms had living quarters for three men, some for five men, and there was a large dormitory for 17 men.

There were hot showers, a cafeteria; and the migrant workers had their own cooks. Every morning, we would bus them out to the fields, and return them around 5:30 PM.

I looked forward to the arrival of these laborers. They were hard workers, and they would get the job done.

We paid them the piece rate established by the United States government. Actually, they were doing quite well, making wages which were above the average of many other workers. That was all right with us, because as I previously stated, they were hard workers. They deserved every dollar we paid them.

Before becoming a Christian, I suppose I treated these workers decent enough; but the truth is, I looked upon them as machines to accomplish the task at hand.

Now, all of a sudden, I had a burden for their souls!

So, I started conducting church services in the labor camps. We would meet once a week in the evenings in the cafeteria.

There was one Jamaican, who was a lay preacher. I enlisted his help to lead singing; and then, we would quote different verses of scripture from the Bible.

The Jamaicans knew the Bible. They had been taught from their mother's knee. Even today, when I meet Jamaicans, I'm astonished at their knowledge of the Bible.

Even if I'm ministering in a Jamaican jail, the prisoners will join in from memory as I begin to quote: *"For God so loved the world that He gave His only begotten Son, that whoever believes in Him should not perish but have everlasting life."*

It always blesses me to hear these men join in as I quote John 3:16, as well as other verses of scripture. Thank God, there's hope for everyone!

Getting back to the labor camps; there were many men who gave their lives to Christ. We would pray for healing; and pray for their families and their needs back in Jamaica.

Because of the change in my heart, I was seeing these workers in a different light; and they began to see me in a different light also! Here were men who had left their families and homeland, and had come thousands of miles to try and provide a better life for them.

Sometimes, we would sit and talk about Jamaica. They would tell me how beautiful it was, and how some day, they hoped I could come for a visit and see for myself.

One day, I came to the camp to check on one of the workers. He was probably our best picker, and I wanted to know why he wasn't working that day.

I was told that another worker had cast a spell upon him!

After our harvest, most of the men would go to Florida to cut sugar cane. Every year, one of the companies down there awarded a belt, studded with silver and semi-precious stones, to the worker who cut the most cane.

This man, who was our best picker, had won the belt, and the other man was jealous.

Some of the Jamaican men asked if I could cast the demon spirit out of this man. The evil spell had made him very sick.

It was my first encounter with Voo Doo; a religion of spiritism, derived from African ancestor worship, and now practiced in various parts of the Caribbean.

We took the man into the cafeteria. The cook and his helper were there, watching us. We stood around the man, laid our hands on his shoulder, and I started to pray, *"in the name of Jesus Christ, come out, you demon spirit. You have no place in this man's life!"*

After several minutes, he starting moaning, twisting and uttering strange sounds. He fell on the floor, and his body started going through all sorts of contortions!

I stood back in awe; amazed at the power and authority in the name of the Lord Jesus Christ!

All these Jamaicans knew exactly what was happening. *"The evil spirit is leaving his body,"* they said!

After a while, the man stood up, as if he were in a daze, and went to his room. The next morning, he was at work; living up to his reputation of being the best picker.

I learned later that the perpetrator of this Voo Doo spell had made an image of the man and pierced it with needles.

Oddly enough, after the man was delivered from this spell, the perpetrator destroyed the image, and the two men became friends!

Since moving to Jamaica, I have encountered Voo Doo on other occasions.

Once up in the mountains, at the end of a service, I noticed two young men standing at the back of the church. One of them explained that he had brought his brother, who had a demon spirit, and he wanted the minister to cast it out. I called the minister, and he joined me in prayer. The same reaction occurred that happened to the man at the labor camp.

Voo Doo is still prevalent in Jamaica. Unfortunately, in some churches it has become mixed with Christianity. Consequently, I have to be on guard during church services, so it doesn't creep in!

At one prayer and fasting meeting, I saw one of the women anoint a man with oil, and began to pray over him. The spirit of Voo Doo was strong in the room, and I observed her casting an evil spirit out of the man.

After her prayer, I explained to the people that the power in the name of Jesus Christ was stronger than all other spirits. The meeting then returned to normal.

At another service, the people began to shout and go around in a daze. They came up on the pulpit, and all sorts of strange things began to happen.

I stopped the service, and the people got upset. They said I had quenched the moving of the Holy Spirit. If it was the Holy Spirit, I didn't recognize it as such! It was satanic! It was the spirit of Voo Doo!

Through the years, I extended the labor camp ministry into other areas, sometimes making 100 mile round trips in the evenings to conduct services.

The workers began to see me, not just as a boss man, but as someone who cared about their well being. Someone who cared about their souls.

Because of my concern for the workers, God opened a door of opportunity for me to serve on the board of directors of a corporation formed by the government to look after the affairs of migrant workers. I was one of a very few employers of migrant workers who was asked to serve in this capacity.

God was using me in many ways. I was always asked to pray at these board meetings. The other members recognized that there was something different about me.

Chapter 13

Ten Years as a Lay Preacher

During one of our weekly Bible studies, a much admired, older lady; one who had dedicated her life to Christ; asked if I would help a certain, little church.

This little church had been established for many years, and was actually an outreach project of our home church.

Unfortunately, the church was located in somewhat of a poverty stricken area. Housing was inadequate; the level of education was low; unemployment was high; and medical benefits were insufficient when compared to the needs of the people!

At one time, this church had been very active; but due to neglect, it had dwindled down to only three or four people.

"Would I come and help," the lady wanted to know?

I told her I had never done anything like this; and furthermore, I didn't know if I was equipped for such a task. But, once again, after much prayer, I agreed to come.

I had once read a book entitled, *"Praying Hyde of India."* One time, this missionary was attending revival meetings in England. It so happened that only a small number of people were coming to the revival; so he suggested to the minister that they pray all day leading up to the evening meeting. That night, the church was full!

This stuck in my mind, so I suggested we call a meeting of the whole community, and explain my purpose in coming. The people in this community knew me only by name. Many of them had worked in the orchards for me or my family. I'm sure it was hard for them to visualize me coming to preach!

On the day of the meeting, I went to the church and prayed from early afternoon until 7:00 that evening, asking God to give me the strength and ability to carry out this assignment.

At 7:00, The lady who asked me to come knocked on the door of the back room where I was praying, and said, *"Randolph, come on out. It's time for the meeting."*

When I walked into the sanctuary, that little church was full! Even a Roman Catholic priest, who I knew, had come to show his support!

The people in this community had every kind of problem you can imagine. Illegitimate births, alcohol, drugs, crime, and perversion!

Of course, we sometimes attribute such problems only to poorer communities; but I've discovered that the same problems exist in affluent communities. The only difference is, they have the means to cover them up!

I started on a temporary basis, visiting people in the community in the evenings after work, and on Saturdays. Some of their homes were not very well kept, and often, I would have to step over trash to get into the house. But, they had warm hearts, and they always made me feel welcome.

On Sundays, we normally had about 25 in attendance. The church building would only hold around 50. A Sunday school was developed for the children; and at every service, I would anoint people with oil, and pray for the sick.

It was always standing room only when we had our Christmas program. I made sure every child received a gift, as well as candy.

In the summer, we had Sunday school picnics at our home. The children would swim in the pool; and we had a big yard in which they could play. I learned to really love these people!

During my time there, I saw the mighty hand of God minister to the needs of these people many times.

One Sunday after church, a woman called to me from across the street, *"Randy, come over here and pray for me."*

She was partly drunk, and sitting on an old, broken down stool. The male friend she was living with, lay next to her on a broken down sofa.

I saw a black man, who I knew, and a few white men, who didn't have the greatest of reputations. I said to them, *"come over here, we're going to pray for our friend!"*

I stepped over mud puddles getting to her porch; and then I said to her male friend, *"put down that whiskey bottle, we're going to pray!"*

I grasped her hands, closed my eyes and began to pray that Jesus would come into her life; and also that she would be delivered from alcoholism. As I was praying, I felt my hands getting wet. She was sobbing, and her tears were falling on my hands.

Within a couple of months, her sister came, and took the woman into her home. She gave her life to Christ, and a few years later, went home to be with Jesus!

One evening, I received a frantic phone call. *"Come quickly, a man has been shot, and they think I did it!"*

As I arrived at the mobile home, a black man ran out and threw his arms around me. *"I thought you would never come,"* he said!

He and two white men had been drinking. While he was preparing some food, one of the white men shot the other one, and ran off. The people of the community saw the black man kneeling over the wounded man, and just assumed that he did it.

After the police arrived, we were able to get things straightened out. The other man was caught and sent to prison.

Another time, when I was on my way to church, this same black man stopped my car. He pleaded with me to come with him to his mother's house. I told him I had to get to the church; that I was already going to be late!

He insisted that I come with him, and I could sense the urgency in his voice. I sent another man to open the church and start the service.

His mother came to the door still dressed in her housecoat. She probably wondered what her son was doing with this white man?

As we all sat around an old, coal burning stove, the man started to cry. He poured out his heart to his mother, explaining that as a black man, he just couldn't make it in life.

His mother tried to encourage him, but he went on and on about how he had been persecuted, and how there was no hope.

Suddenly, he pulled out a revolver, and stuck it to his head!

Without thinking, I grabbed for his hand. Off the chair we went; the stove was knocked over; coal dust went everywhere!

I had seen this man's uncle, who was a large man, out mowing the yard. I shouted for the mother to get him!

As we continued to struggle, he pointed the gun at me! Finally, when his uncle came, we wrenched the gun from his hand!

The man ran out of the house crying. I ran after him, following him to the wood pile. *"Why on earth did you ask me to come here with you,"* I asked?

"I wanted someone to pray for me after I shot myself," was his reply!

The next day, we went up to one of my mountain orchards to pray. He received Christ into his life, and started coming to church.

He wanted to give me something to show his appreciation. It was a cross he had made from match sticks, the ends burnt, and glued to pop sickle sticks.

As I write this book, I'm looking at that cross! It reminds me to pray for him. Unfortunately, he's serving time in prison for drugs.

A big, strapping, black man charged into the church, shouting and cursing at the top of his voice, *"you better come get that S.O.B. before I kill him!"*

I looked him square in the eyes. *"This is God's house,"* I said! *"We're having service now, and afterwards, we'll talk!"*

He quietly sat down, and we continued the service. Then, at the end of the service, he stood and asked to share a testimony in song!

I agreed, and I have never; either before or since; heard the *"Lord's Prayer"* sang so beautifully! He had a deep, baritone voice, and could have been a professional singer with a little training.

After the service, I went with him to see his son, who was involved in drugs. Things quieted down in their home, and occasionally, I would see the man in church.

Even today, whenever I see this man, he always speaks to me. When I ask him about his relationship with God, he says he's going to church. Hopefully, he has a real relationship with God!

The telephone rang. *"Please come to the hospital, my son is dying,"* the voice pleaded!

When I arrived, I found one of my best workers, who had lived with a certain woman, off and on, for a number of years. It was an interracial love affair.

I laid my hand upon the young boy, and requested that the mother lay her hand upon mine. As I was praying, I felt another hand upon mine. It was the man who called me!

I told the mother to call me, no matter what time it was, when she had further news. It was around midnight when I left. Three hours later, the phone rang. *"Randy, my son is better. Right after you left, the fever began to leave his body, and he started talking!"*

God answers prayer! Don't ever, ever stop praying!

"I want to talk with you," the man said as I was coming out of church. He began to pour out the most perverse sexual story I've ever heard. He even had sex with animals!

I said, *"you don't need to tell this to me. Get in that church, fall on your knees, confess your sins before God, and ask for his mercy!"*

Every Sunday, I would go by the labor camp and bring some of the Jamaican men to the services. The church had been given a good, used organ, and a lady from the mother church would come by and play for us. Those Jamaican men would make the church ring with their singing!

A cross from Jamaica still hangs in the front of the church.

I had dedicated ten years into the lives of these people. I had walked with them through their sufferings, rejoiced with them in their joy.

I had watched as their kids grew up, attended college, got married, and became good citizens. I had buried their loved ones!

But now, my heart had changed. I was feeling the call of God to Jamaica!

At my farewell dinner, I believe the entire community was there! The kids clung to me, and wouldn't let me go! A beautiful cake was presented with the words inscribed on top, *"God Bless Your Work In Jamaica!"*

A very rough man; who worked for me, and occasionally came to church; showed up at the door. He came over, squatted beside me, and began to tell me all I meant to him, his friends, and the community.

He was an Indian, who had been raised on a reservation in Minnesota. I had buried his girlfriend, and he had given me a pair of infant sized moccasins as a gift.

After photographs were taken, the people presented me with a half gallon jar, which was full of money that had been deposited through a slit in the lid. When I got home and counted the money, there was over $120.00.

All those ten years, I know God was carefully and precisely preparing me for the work in Jamaica. As I look back, and reflect upon those years, I'm so thankful I obeyed God. The lessons I learned then have been invaluable to my ministry in Jamaica!

Whenever I go back to the states, I try to visit that little church, for it was there that God worked out his purposes for my life!

More than anything, I'm just blessed to be a servant of God. I have no formal education, as far as the ministry is concerned. I had no special training, except by the Holy Spirit. Yet, God chose to use me.

My encouragement to you is this, *"when you hear the Lord's voice, be obedient, and you will be blessed! It doesn't matter how unqualified you think you are; and it doesn't matter how old you are! Just obey the voice of the Lord, and he will use you mightily!"*

Chapter 14

Prepared for the Mission Field

Let me regress for a while, and continue sharing how the Lord prepared me for the ministry; and ultimately, the mission field of Jamaica. And remember, this was at a time in my life when most people are preparing for an entirely different event; namely, retirement!

Some friends invited us to a meeting of the Full Gospel Business Men's Fellowship. This particular meeting was in Winchester, Virginia. At the time, I had never heard of this organization; but someone gave me a book entitled, *"The Happiest People on Earth."* The book was written by the founder.

Well, I literally could not put that book down. It was so very interesting and exciting!

Anyway, Trudee and I agreed to go to this meeting, but we decided to take our own car. If things got out of hand, we could make a quick exit! I wasn't sure how these meetings would line up with my Presbyterian doctrine.

About halfway to the meeting, our automobile experienced some engine trouble, so I said to our friends who were following us, *"just go on without us!"*

Well, they would have none of that, so we ended up riding with them. So much for my escape plans!

I have never seen so much joy! There must have been 300 people at the meeting; and everyone was hugging like they hadn't seen one another in years.

The speaker was a former military man named Johnny Johnson, who at that time was the most decorated black man in U.S. history!

As he walked into the room, there seemed to be a glow about him. He gave a powerful message that night, about how he overcame the obstacles of life with God's love. Many went forward for salvation and healing. Little did I know that one day, he would become a close friend.

Afterwards, I was checking the book table to see if there were any books by Presbyterians. I wanted to know if my church agreed with this type of meeting. I found a book by Peter Marshall, Jr. That made me feel better!

Despite my initial apprehension, the truth is, that meeting changed my life! I began to attend FGBMFI meetings all over the area. I just couldn't get enough of these meetings!

In the process of time, some friends and I started a chapter in our town. Our meetings were equally exciting, and we always attracted large crowds. We invited the biggest name speakers in the charismatic movement.

One such speaker was Johnny Johnson. I remember the time he and I drove up to my mountain orchard to pray. Another time, I visited him in Washington, D.C., when he was working for the government.

Eventually, I became a field director for the FGBMFI. This put me into contact with many influential Christians. A large number of these people have remained my friends throughout the years; and some of them were my only source of support when I first moved to Jamaica.

God did so many wonderful things in those meetings. Lack of space does not permit me to share all of them, but I'll share one very significant event.

One evening as I was driving home from one of our chapter meetings, I saw a young man walking out of town. I recognized him, because I had just seen him at our meeting. It was raining, so I picked him up.

As we drove along, we talked about different things; but before he got out of the car, he confessed to me that he was a homosexual.

I invited him to our home for dinner the next evening. Hopefully, my wife and I would be able to minister to him.

We ended up sponsoring him to attend a Christian retreat where there was a strong emphasis on ministering to homosexual men; specifically to restore them to a heterosexual lifestyle.

Over the years, I lost track of him; but one time when I was visiting in the states, I ran into him. He looked great, and took me to meet his wife!

I'm just amazed, not only about how God prepared me, but also, how he provided for every little detail of my eventual ministry in Jamaica!

Many times, I was invited to be a guest on Christian Television, WLYJ in the Clarksburg, West Virginia area. The manager there has become a close friend, and has been a great blessing to my ministry in Jamaica.

I've developed many other close relationships in the Clarksburg/Fairmont area, as well as other areas of West Virginia. The names are too numerous to mention; but a number of these people have come to Jamaica on work teams. Others have provided tremendous support for my ministry in different ways.

He was about 15 years old. He had been living outside of town in a field, but came into town to find odd jobs in order to survive.

At one home where he was working, he stole some items from a garage; and was sent to the local jail. Subsequently, he was given the chance to live with a Christian family, instead of serving a jail sentence.

One evening, this young boy, and the family with whom he was living, came to visit. He had become somewhat attached to me. We had developed a relationship at church.

Well, he wanted to come live with us; and after talking over the matter, it was mutually agreed that he be allowed to do so. I could provide employment for him in the orchards.

My son was living away from home at the time; my daughter was attending university. So, there was no problem with my children. But, we had no idea of the adventures that awaited us!

Even though this young boy had a sordid and scarred past, my wife treated him just like he was her own son!

He was not one to display affection, but one night when I was in the hospital, he came by to visit. He thought I was unconscious, so he bent down and kissed me on the cheek. I believe it was his way of showing appreciation in case I didn't recover.

One night; while I was still recuperating at home; he came in to see me. He was very upset! He had learned that his father; who was visiting from Baltimore; was not his real father! This man had married his mother after she was already pregnant.

Nevertheless, he continued a relationship with this man, who eventually persuaded him to come to Baltimore to work.

Sometime later, one evening close to Christmas, he called me from a nearby town. He wanted to come by and deliver Christmas gifts to Trudee and myself.

It was very cold at this time of the year, but when he arrived, he was poorly dressed and had no coat. The more he talked, the more I became convinced that he was either drinking, or on drugs. I couldn't help but notice the marks on his arms where he had been shooting up drugs!

He said a friend was waiting for him in the car. They had a gun, and they were planning on holding up a drug store!

I said to him, *"young man, I'm going to give you some money and some food, and I want you to go straight back to Baltimore tonight!"*

Unfortunately, the next day's headlines in the newspaper revealed that a drug store in a nearby town had been held up. This young boy and his friend had been apprehended!

I visited him in jail, and strangely enough, he was released into my custody, and allowed to come back home with me!

He stayed close to home for a while; but one night, I mistakenly allowed him to go into town. I waited up for him until past midnight. When he finally got home, he was all bloody and badly beaten due to a fight.

He was determined to go back into town for revenge, but I ordered him to get cleaned up and go to bed.

When he came out of the bathroom, he was violent! He had a chain blade from a chain saw, and was swirling it around, and demanding that I get out of his way!

I stood in the door of our house, refusing to let him pass. He came at me full force, still swirling that chain around. Strangely enough, he tripped on his own shoe laces, and I was able to take the chain away from him!

He ran out the door, jumped into my car, and drove off. Somehow, he had gotten a set of my keys. I called the police, and they set up a roadblock and stopped him just outside of Romney.

He spent that night in the local Romney jail; but the next day, two Christian brothers and I had to return him to the jail from which he had been released into my custody after the robbery.

Turning that boy over to the authorities was one of the hardest things I ever had to do! He was sentenced to a prison term.

I've learned that many times you have to release a person into God's hands, and let him work out his purpose for their lives.

One evening, I received a phone call from a prison in Ohio. It was this young man. He insisted that he was now a Christian. He said his life was changed, and he was now attending church services.

I didn't know if this was a con job or not, so I just said, "*I hope so!*"

This all happened in the early 1980's; but just a little over a year ago, when I was appearing on a Christian television program in the states, this man called the station.

He told me he was married, had a child, and was driving a tractor trailer for a living. Furthermore, he told me that he had become a committed Christian, and watched this program on a regular basis.

He couldn't believe that it was actually me on the program. He encouraged me to keep up the good work, emphasizing that I didn't realize how many lives I was touching!

"Through the Lord's mercies we are not consumed, because His compassions fail not. They are new every morning; great is Your faithfulness!" (Lamentations 3:22-23).

During those years, we had several other people stay with us for various reasons, and for various lengths of time.

I had no idea that God was training me for one of the most important phases of my ministry in Jamaica. To the best of my ability, I was just reaching out to hurting people with the compassion of God!

Chapter 15

The Winds of Change

At the height of our business, we owned 2,000 acres of land, upon which were 1,000 acres of orchards. We leased another 200 acres of orchards.

We had cold storage facilities of 56,000 square feet that would hold 180,000 bushels of fruit; including a storage room that would keep apples fresh the year round.

We had a packing facility that operated 10 months out of the year. We were shipping fruit all over the eastern United States, as well as exporting fruit to Europe, and operating a Christmas gift box trade.

There were numerous tractors, trailers, trucks and buses, with two garages to keep them operational.

We operated two labor camps, and had a full-time employee force of 50 people, which increased to 150 during harvest time.

In addition, we sold chemicals, fertilizers, and farm supplies to other growers.

Despite a very busy schedule, I remained faithful to the Lord. Every morning, I got up at 5:00 AM for Bible reading and prayer; reading through the Bible once every year. All of this served to bring me into a closer relationship with God, becoming one with him, as Jesus prayed in John 17:21.

And, God showed himself strong in our business. One of our orchards was located on the side of a mountain. In the summer, hail storms would sometimes sweep through the area, and it was not unusual for this mountain orchard to receive heavy damage.

After I became a Christian, I would anoint this orchard, and pray over it; praying specifically that no hail storm would come near it!

One evening, we had a severe hail storm in that area. Afterwards, I drove over to see what damage we might have received. The road leading to the orchard was literally covered with leaves, twigs and limbs. One would have thought the damage was severe.

However, as I came closer to the orchard, I strangely noticed an absence of debris. I could not find even one damaged apple!

Then, in 1978, something happened that would eventually change the entire course of my life. My wife and I made our first visit to Jamaica!

We went down with a group of growers, who like us, were using Jamaicans for their harvest. We attended meetings at luxurious hotels with representatives of the Jamaican government. Of course, the purpose of the meetings was to stimulate the farm program that brought upwards of eight to ten thousand Jamaican workers to the United States on a yearly basis.

One evening, the Prime Minister attended a meeting. There was a big reception for him in the hotel gardens. A Kingston military band was on hand to provide music. A Jamaican lady; who had received voice training in the states; provided us with a beautiful solo.

As we were going through the reception line to meet the Prime Minister, I shook hands with the lady who had performed the solo. I told her how much I enjoyed her song; and almost before I realized it, I said, *"I also see something else very special about you!"*

She inquired as to what else I saw in her? I replied, *"I see Jesus Christ in you!"*

This had to be God, because this type of thing was totally out of character for me!

With that, she took me by the arm, pulled me out of the reception line, and began introducing me to the government officials as her new Christian friend!

She asked me to come to a breakfast the next morning to speak to a group of Christians who worked for the Prime Minister. One man who attended the breakfast was the Assistant Secretary of Labor.

The day we were preparing for our return to the states, I felt the Holy Spirit prompting me to go and pray for this man.

This was a bold move on my part, but I obeyed God. I knocked on the door of his hotel suite, and told the maid I that wished to talk with the Secretary.

He was very gracious when he learned that I had come to pray. I prayed for Jamaica, I prayed for the government, and I prayed for him! To this day, we have remained friends.

Little did I know that God was preparing me to minister in that nation; but I did know that I had fallen in love with Jamaica!

There was a Jamaican minister who worked for me during harvest time. He invited me to attend a conference he was holding at his church.

It was there that I first saw the other side of Jamaica; the hunger and suffering of multitudes of poor people!

At one service, a woman came forward with a baby. She asked me to pray for her, stating that all she had to feed her baby was sugar water. She was speaking specifically of water that was squeezed out of sugar cane!

I have never forgotten the look on her face. When I departed, she gave me a bottle of small sea shells that she had laboriously gathered to show her appreciation!

Back at the orchards, things changed. I started a small group that met every morning for prayer before beginning the day's work.

I had a large, red, apple plaque made, with an inscription below it, *"Keep my commands and live, and my law as the apple of your eye."* (Proverbs 7:2). I hung the plaque in the outer office where business was conducted with the public. Quite a few customers commented on it!

I didn't permit cursing or profanity on the job; and oddly enough, I found the workers very responsive! Many of them came to me for prayer about their problems.

The entire atmosphere about me seemed to be changing, not just at work, but also at home, and in my social life. I found that I was not attending as many social functions; and the friends I once had were drifting further away! When I did attend social functions, I was almost always asked to say a blessing before meals!

Often, when I was conducting business, a question on morals or ethics would arise. My business associates; some of whom I had known for years; would say, *"ask Randolph, he's the preacher!"*

I served on the board of directors for a large apple juice cooperative. When the board met, there was never a mention of prayer prior to the meetings. My spirit convicted me that this was wrong, and I approached the president and discussed my concern with him.

At the next board meeting my proposal was voted upon. I was very apprehensive, but it passed unanimously. From that time, I was always asked to open meetings with a prayer! When you're bold with your witness for Christ, he will always honor it!

Trudee and I continued to go to Jamaica every year. In 1982, we were invited by one of my Jamaican workers to his parish, which was near Negril, on the west coast of Jamaica.

At this time, Negril was a quiet place to relax. Today, it's the fastest growing resort area in Jamaica; and unfortunately, is known for its promiscuousness, nude beaches, and open sin!

Our worker, Fred found us a nice, little cottage by the sea where we could relax and go for a swim. Each day, we would take a taxi to Fred's house, and visit with him and his family. They invited their neighbors to come and hear the word of God; and after several days, 12 of them gave their lives to Christ.

I had brought some New Testaments with me on this trip; and I still have a photograph of these new believers standing by a grove of banana trees with their New Testaments in their hands.

When we were preparing to return to the states, God spoke to me about appointing a Bible study leader over the group, so that they might continue.

I had no idea who to appoint. I thought about Fred, but said, *"no, Lord, he's an immature Christian. He still grows ganja in the hills for extra money."*

I thought about Fred's brother. He was formerly a Rastafarian, but had just given his life to Christ. He was obviously too young!

Not knowing who to appoint, I put a fleece before the Lord. I said, *"Lord, whoever comes to bid us good-bye in the morning, that's who I will appoint!"*

The next morning, no one came to bid us goodbye! We took a private taxi back to the airport in Montego Bay. As we drove along, I kept asking God, *"why didn't you send someone?"*

When we arrived at the airport, we discovered that our flight had been delayed. We cleared Customs and Immigration, and were sent to a secure area to wait for our flight. Security guards prohibited outsiders from entering this area.

I was standing, looking out at the runway, wondering why God didn't send someone. I heard a voice speak to me, *"Randolph, turn around and see who is here!"*

As I whirled around, much to my surprise, there stood Fred and his wife. I asked, *"Fred, how did you get here?"*

He replied, *"Mr. Randy, the car that was bringing us to say good-bye broke down; so we caught a bus here to Montego Bay. I kept praying that you had not already left!"*

My next question was, *"how did you get into this secure area?"*

"Oh," he said, *"I just told them that my boss man was in there; and that I had missed telling them good-bye; and that I had driven 70 miles, praying that they had not yet left!"*

At that time, the Lord spoke to me, *"Fred is the man!"*

I knew that they had likely spent most of their money to purchase the bus tickets; and I understood that the delay had been arranged by God!

We moved to a private area, and I shared with Fred how God had shown me that he was the leader of this group of new Christians.

I explained to him the importance of instructing these new believers. I anointed him with oil, prayed over him; and asked him to stay in touch with me, keeping me informed of the progress of the group.

Later, as we were sitting on the runway, preparing to take off, I felt a strange feeling come over me. I knew God was speaking to me. I turned to my wife, and said, *"Trudee, I believe God is showing me that some rough times await us when we arrive home!"*

God was not only alerting me, but also preparing me for the greatest change thus far in my entire life!

Chapter 16

The End of an Era

    I was looked upon as one of the more progressive businessmen in the area; one who had started with very little, but had become successful. Our fruit growing business was doing really well, and we were experiencing growth every year.

    However, after returning from our latest trip to Jamaica, it seemed like God removed his hand of blessing from the business!

    Interest rates began climbing, increasing from 7% to 18%. We were having difficulty paying off the loans we acquired on a yearly basis to help operate the business.

Suddenly, hail storms were becoming a problem! In the absence of storms, drought became a problem. Instead of making money, we were losing $200,000.00 or more a year.

I considered myself a good businessman. I plugged every hole I could, but to no avail!

My partners wanted out, but I still thought I could turn the business around. I began buying up my partner's stock and eventually acquired over 75% of the business. By the next season however, things had become so bad that I had to sell some of the properties!

Meanwhile, my daughter was planning to get married. I had always promised her a big wedding with a champagne fountain, catered food, and all the trimmings.

We decided to substitute a non-alcoholic, sparkling, apple champagne in the fountain. Quite a few of our guests would be Christians, and we didn't want to offend them.

It was a beautiful wedding. The church was literally filled with flowers. Afterwards, we held the reception at our home. A large tent was erected in the yard for serving food; there was a huge wedding cake; and of course, the apple champagne fountain!

The trees in our yard were uniquely decorated with cotton doves, which were filled with rice for showering the bride and groom when they departed for their honeymoon!

There were hundreds of helium filled balloons, which were released at the close of all the festivities.

Last, but not least, there was live music, and valet parking.

It was our last, big Hurrah!

In 1985, one of the worst floods to ever hit our area came pouring down the Potomac river, overflowing its banks, and rushing into our cold storage and packing house!

The harvest was almost finished. Many of the workers had gone. The cold storage holding lot was completely filled with over 10,000 bushels of apples.

It had been raining for two days; and in the evening before retiring, I told Trudee that we should pray for the people that lived along the river. It appeared that we were going to have some serious flooding!

The next morning as I was shaving, the telephone rang. *"Randolph, you better come quick! The river is up to the cold storage and beginning to enter the building!"*

I went back to shaving. I couldn't believe the river was actually that high. The biggest flood we ever experienced was in 1936, and it just came up to where the cold storage was built. In fact, that's why we built the building in that location! Supposedly, It was out of the flood zone!

Our cold storage had three floors. On the bottom floor, we had refrigeration machinery, a packing house, and a special storage room for keeping apples the year round.

There was another storage room on this bottom floor where a truck had just unloaded 5,000 cardboard boxes for packing fruit. At the time, there were about 40,000 bushels of apples on this floor!

The second floor consisted of my office, a sales office, storage space for fertilizers and chemicals; plus, storage space for another 40,000 bushels of apples.

The third floor consisted entirely of apple storage space.

I maneuvered my four wheel drive vehicle as close as possible. Water had covered the highway; state troopers weren't allowing anyone to pass; traffic was backed up! I waded through knee deep water the rest of the way!

Water had covered the holding lot, and was rising. I could see apples beginning to float down the river.

I could hear the fly wheels of the big compressors that ran our refrigeration units going, *"Thump, Thump, Thump!"* I quickly moved to turn them off, but when I got to the stairs leading down to where they were located, the water was too deep!

By now, most of the 10,000 bushels of apples in the holding lot had floated away! Loud speakers from police cars encouraged people to evacuate the area.

I thought about my brother who had a farm adjacent to the storage. As I looked out the window, I could see cattle, barns, and parts of houses floating down the river!

Loud speakers from the police cars were now calling to me, *"get out of the building!"* I escaped by jumping onto a bank of earth that supported the highway. I waded through ever deepening waters until I was able to climb up over the bank and onto the highway!

The next day, after the waters had somewhat subsided, I went down to the storage. I just stood there, numb and in shock!

All the vehicles: trucks, tractors, buses, had been submerged in water! Every motor and moving part would have to be cleaned and rebuilt!

Even the empty bins on the holding lot had been washed down the river!

I couldn't get into the building. Mud was half way up to my knees, and covered everything!

Some of the workers stood around, and asked what we were going to do? I said, *"the first thing we're going to do is shovel the mud away from the doors, so we can get into the building!"*

The water had risen nine feet in storage rooms that had eleven foot ceilings. Water had covered over 40,000 bushels of apples. They were now covered with mud and strewn everywhere!

Everything was caked with mud: conveyor belts; refrigeration equipment; the huge, three phase electric panel boxes! Without refrigeration, it was just a matter of days before the apples on the second and third floors spoiled!

The 5,000 cardboard, packing boxes that had been recently delivered were all ruined!

The bottom line; it looked like we had lost everything!

I walked out of the building, tears streaming down my cheeks. I looked toward heaven, and said, *"Lord, is this all there is after 43 years of hard work?"*

I felt an arm upon my shoulder. It was my son. *"Dad,"* he said, *"it will be all right. Somehow, we'll make it!"* Oh, how I needed to hear those words at this time!

We worked night and day to get back into operation. Within two weeks, the power was finally restored, and we began packing the remaining apples. I would come home at night, dead tired, with mud all over me! My wife would wash me down with the garden hose before I could enter the house!

The effects of the flood were devastating! Over 50 lives lost; and many homes and untold amounts of livestock washed down the river. Several towns were almost completely washed away!

Many disaster relief organizations came to help. The government set up a disaster relief loan program. Our loss had exceeded $500,000.00, with no insurance!

I applied for a loan; but with the heavy debt load we were already carrying, and the tremendous losses we had suffered, it was the beginning of the end! It seemed like the final nail had been driven into the coffin!

We managed to harvest two more crops, but we were facing an almost impossible, uphill struggle.

I investigated a payment plan where I could restructure our debt over a number of years. When I figured it out, I told the loan officer that I would never live long enough to see the debt paid. I decided it was time to close the business!

I began selling the real estate privately. I was able to sell all of the property except two small parcels; one a wooded area, and the other which housed one of our labor camps.

The cold storage and all of our equipment was to be sold at auction. There would be a lot of interest in this type of sale, and we had high hopes that it would generate quite a lot of money.

I got up early in the morning, and had my quiet time with the Lord. I knew that he was directing my path, although right now, things were very difficult!

I had decided to operate a concession at the auction, and all the profits would go to the ministry in Jamaica.

Later that morning, when I arrived at the storage, all the vehicles and equipment were lined up and everything was being made ready for the sale. For a few moments, I sadly reflected on all the time, labor and money that had gone into my life's work.

I quickly turned my attention back to the concession stand, and delivered the supplies to the people I had hired to operate it.

I asked the Lord for strength to be a good witness. Many would be watching to see how I reacted. This was the end of an era! Three generations of fruit growers being closed out!

It was one of the biggest farm sales of the area. More than 600 people came, and the sale lasted from 9:00 AM until 6:00 PM.

I was sitting in the office during the sale. The wife of a close friend came over an kissed me on the cheek, said nothing, and hurriedly left! She understood the hurt. Not many did!

The sale grossed over $300,000.00. It was quickly dispersed to the bank as payment on our farm loan.

The concession made $300.00 for the ministry work in Jamaica.

The next day, I sat quietly in my office. I thought back to the many years of rising at 5:00 AM. I thought about the many sleepless nights worrying over the crops and the debts.

And then, suddenly, a startling realization came over me! I WAS FREE! I was free to serve the Lord without all the encumbrances that for so long had dominated my life!

The new owners of the storage offered me a job until I was 65, when I would begin drawing social security.

I told them I wanted a month off. Trudee and I began to pack. I was going to Jamaica to discover what God wanted me to do!

Chapter 17

Jamaica Calls

I really believed God was calling me to Jamaica, but I didn't have the slightest idea about what part of the island.

2 Samuel 2:1 says, *"....David inquired of the Lord, saying, Shall I go up to any of the cities of Judah? And the Lord said to him, Go up. David said, Where shall I go up? And He said, to Hebron."*

So, I prayed, *"Lord, shall Randolph go up to any of the cities of Jamaica?"*

And the Lord would answer, *"go up!"*

Then, I would ask, *"Lord, unto which city shall I go up?"*

There was no answer, only go to Jamaica; but I knew God would show the way!

I hired one of my former Jamaican workers to drive us all over Jamaica. He had an old, run down car, but other than a flat tire or so, we managed to cover the island.

In Kingston, we stayed at the same hotel where I helped to start a chapter of the *"Full Gospel Business Men's Fellowship."*

I thought it would be good for Trudee to meet some of my Christian acquaintances in Kingston, so we arranged a little reception for about 30 people.

One of those present at the reception was Dr. V. T. Williams, who was the founder of an organization called the Jamaican Evangelistic Center. He had established eleven churches throughout the island, as well as a day school for over 100 children.

He worked with the poor and uneducated; and these were the people to whom God was calling me!

As the reception was ending, one of the ladies said to me, *"why don't you go up to Mandeville? Dr. V. T. has a church there that you may be interested in!"*

I didn't see how we could possibly go. We were scheduled to return to the states the next day. Then, I heard a little voice inside of me say, *"go up to Mandeville!"*

Isaiah 30:21 says, *"Your ears shall hear a word behind you, saying, This is the way, walk in it...."*

We were very impressed with Mandeville. It's in the mountains, at an elevation of about 3,000 feet. Consequently, the temperature is about 10 degrees cooler than the lower areas.

My driver and I visited a church that night which was supposed to be affiliated with the Jamaican Evangelistic Association. However, we were informed that the church had broken away from this organization. *(splits, divisions and breakaways are common in Jamaica)!* We were given directions to a small church about three miles down the mountain.

We parked in front of this little, store front church, which had formerly been both a dance hall and a garage! It was in a very poor area; but there were at least four bars within sight! Many young men and girls were strolling the streets, looking for adventure!

After waiting around for a while, a big, old car drove up to the front of the church, and out stepped a large, Jamaican woman.

Sister Brown, or *"Missionary Brown,"* as she was sometimes called, was the leader of the church. There were lots of children, some teenagers, and a precious few adults.

The moment I walked into the church, I knew this was where God had called me!

I was invited to sit on the platform that night, so I got a good look at the interior of the church. It was basically four bare walls, a concrete floor, and a rusty, tin roof. I couldn't help but notice all the repair work that was needed.

I was asked to deliver a greeting to the people; which to most Jamaicans means a mini-sermon! I took a few photographs; and told them that one day, I would be returning!

Back at the hotel, I excitedly told Trudee, *"this is the place where God has called me! I said, Lord, should Randolph go up to Mandeville? And the Lord said to me, Go up!"*

I wanted very much to go to Jamaica as a missionary sent out by my church; but I quickly learned that such a desire was not possible unless I went to four years of Bible school.

I was a bit disheartened. I was 64 years old at the time. If I spent the next four years in Bible school, I might not have enough time left to fulfill what God had called me to do!

And, who knows; after graduating from Bible school, my church may have decided that I was too old to go! I knew I must be obedient to God!

So, I worked a few months for the new owners of the cold storage, until I was 65; and then, I made plans to leave for Jamaica.

I acquired a one year work permit through the Jamaican Evangelistic Association; but when we left in January, 1989, I knew I was changing professions forever!

When we arrived at the Kingston Airport; sent out by nobody, except God; we had with us, six pieces of luggage, $1,000.00 in cash, and nothing else!

We waited three hours in the hot, tropical sun before someone from the church picked us up! In Jamaica, you have to learn a little patience if you want to survive. Jamaican time is not quite so punctual as what we're used to in the states!

Sister Brown had rented us a house, and placed some of her own furniture in it. When we first moved in, the electricity had not been turned on; and there was no gas for cooking. We began to think, maybe this was not our calling after all!

The next day, however, the current was turned on; and we obtained a bottle of cooking gas. For now, we were in business!

We had no transportation, so I walked a mile to a shopping area, bought groceries, and walked the mile back home!

We were completely alone. Other than Sister Brown, we didn't know another soul in Mandeville.

The island of Jamaica is over 90% black. I was beginning to understand how a black person living in a white community in the U.S. must feel!

If God calls you as a missionary, and you have any attitudes of racism, you best get rid of them quickly!

Sister Brown's car was being overhauled, and she was having difficulty coming up with the money for the repair bill. I suggested that I would pay half, if she would allow us to use the car when she wasn't using it.

This arrangement worked out rather well. We now had transportation to buy groceries, and go into town. We even took a few, little, side trips to see some of the island. God was taking care of us!

The first Sunday, Dr. V. T. Williams was to be at the church to introduce me. We were to be picked up at 11:00 AM.

Well, 11:00 came, and went! I told Trudee they must have forgotten. I decided to walk down to a nearby Moravian church for services. *"If anyone comes,"* I told her, *"just send them to the church to pick me up."*

I came home after the services. No one had come! I changed into my casual clothes, and we had lunch.

Then, at 2:00 in the afternoon, a car pulled up to the house. The driver had come to take me to the church. I thought, *"surely, he must be joking!"* But no, he insisted that I must come; the people were waiting! I must say, this was one of the more extreme cases of Jamaican time that I have experienced!

We still had a house in West Virginia, and that summer, we went back to look after it; promising to return to Jamaica in the Fall.

Before leaving, two white ladies came by. They and their husbands were missionaries. One of them said she and her husband had been called to another Caribbean area; and they were going to sell their furniture and van.

They wanted $5,000.00 *(U.S.)* for the furniture, and $16,000.00 *(U.S.)* for a 15 passenger van. Such prices seemed high when compared to similar items in the states; but in Jamaica, they were reasonable because of customs, and the cost of shipping.

I soon learned that almost everything in Jamaica; except for the local foods; is more expensive than the states. Everything has to be shipped in!

Trudee and I discussed the matter. We honestly did not have that much money. All we had left was our home and a little savings. However, when I prayed, the Lord spoke to me to buy both the furniture and the van!

I told this couple we would send them a down payment of $2,000.00 when we got home, and the rest by the first of August. If I didn't send the balance, they could have the down payment, and we would be the losers! They accepted!

We also made arrangements to rent the house where they were living. The furniture and the van could be left right where it was! When we came back in the fall, we would be ready to dive right into our missionary work! It's amazing how God provides for our needs!

The orchards that we once owned overlooked the town of Romney, West Virginia. It was one of the most panoramic views in that region.

When the apples were in bloom, we left the road open so people could drive up and enjoy the blossoms and the view.

Once, after the U.S. and China had reestablished relations, the Ambassador to China brought a large delegation of Chinese to enjoy the view.

I had sold the property to a real estate developer, who had subdivided it into 99 lots of two or more acres. I asked if I could help sell the lots? The developer thought it was a good idea, since I knew the property better than anyone.

By August, when I was planning to return to Jamaica, I had made over $13,000.00 in commissions. Not bad for an inexperienced, first time salesman! I outsold all the other salesmen! God is good!

Trudee sold her small station wagon for $2,000.00. Various churches, which had me come and share, gave around $4,000.00 in offerings. Another $2,000.00 was given by Christian friends. We had been obedient to God, and he had provided the money to pay off our obligation for the furniture and van!

When we arrived back in Jamaica, it was a real blessing to immediately have a furnished home and a van. Everyday, we used that van; hauling people to church; conducting business in town; and traveling to other parts of the island for speaking engagements.

God was using us!

Chapter 18

My Jamaican Son

At the church there was a young man by the name of O'Neil Sherman. We didn't know it at the time, but he was to become a very vital part of our lives! He was working with the young people in the church, and we could see the love of God in him.

Not long after we arrived in Mandeville, he came by the house. *"How can a young man work for the Lord, and still keep his life pure,"* he wanted to know?

I read Psalm 119:9 to him, *"How can a young man cleanse his way? By taking heed according to your word!"*

We talked for a long time, and prayed together. I encouraged him to enroll in a 100 hour Bible class at the Jamaican Bible College in Mandeville. The classes were held in the evenings, so he could continue his work as an automobile mechanic during the days.

He finished the course, and came back for more. He wanted to go on with the Lord!

Youth With A Mission was located about 12 miles from Mandeville. I told O'Neil that when we returned from the states, we would see what arrangements could be made.

Actually, I made a deal with him. I told him if he would come up with half the tuition for the YWAM Discipleship Training Program, I would pay the other half!

Meanwhile, that second summer, we had to make a trip back to West Virginia because of the home we still owned there.

We needed to make a decision about the house. We could sell it, or maybe rent it; but we could not continue to maintain two homes and be completely faithful to God! Matthew 6:24 says, *"No one can serve two masters; for either he will hate the one and love the other, or else he will be loyal to the one and despise the other. You cannot serve God and mammon!"*

We put the house on the market. Many people came and looked, but no one could afford the price.

After the listing period ended, I decided to sell it myself. One day as I was praying, the Lord impressed upon me to offer the home to a man who had worked for me as a youth.

He was now in the car business, and was doing quite well; but he said there was no way he could afford to buy our home!

Fortunately, we were able to structure a finance plan that benefited both him and us. The sale of the house proved to be a great blessing, providing us with additional income, which we sorely needed!

After the sale of our home, there remained one more item of business, and this was the hardest of all. I'm speaking of the sale of our furniture and personal belongings!

Many pieces of our furniture were family heirlooms, some dating back to the 1700's. Also, through the years of our marriage, we had collected antiques, china, sterling silver, crystal and paintings that were not only valuable, but very dear to us.

Fortunately, a few years earlier, God had taught us a very valuable lesson about the uncertainty of riches. We were visiting with our daughter, who lived in the Chicago area, when we received an urgent phone call.

Our home had been burglarized! All of our sterling silver, china, crystal and paintings had been stolen. Also missing was a personal collection of mechanical banks.

I shook when I heard the news. Trudee took the news better than I. She said we may as well finish our visit, because we couldn't change a thing!

The loss was staggering! In addition to those losses described to us over the phone, various other pieces of furniture, antiques and other valuables were missing. The loss was probably around $50,000.00!

The police took fingerprints. I began to visit antique shops within a 100 mile radius to see if any of our things showed up for sale. We put ads in antique magazines, offering a reward. All to no avail!

Gradually, we coped with the loss, returning to everyday dishes and stainless steel eating utensils. Trudee rearranged the furniture so that the losses wouldn't be so obvious.

The scriptures that sustained me through this time of difficulty were Matthew 6:19-21, *"Do not lay up for yourselves treasures on earth, where moth and rust destroy and where thieves break in and steal; but lay up for yourselves treasures in heaven, where neither moth nor rust destroys and where thieves do not break in and steal. For where your treasure is, there your heart will be also!"*

Of course, God didn't cause the theft; but he used this opportunity to demonstrate to us the emptiness of seeking fulfillment, or establishing our security in things! We learned that fulfillment and security is found in our relationship with God, and obedience to his will!

Six months later, an absolutely amazing thing happened. Early one Sunday morning, my older brother excitedly came up the hill to our home. *"Randolph,"* he shouted, *"come quickly, your stolen property is stacked in the driveway down by the entrance gate!"*

Down the hill I ran! Sure enough, there was everything, stacked in the driveway. I could hardly believe my eyes! A note was attached, *"I'm sorry, please forgive me. I hope it's all here!"* I was reminded of the old saying, *"God works in miraculous ways, his wonders to perform!"*

They never did catch the thief; but one day a few months later, I was washing my car when a friend drove up. He said, *"Randolph, I need to talk with you!"*

"Go ahead," I replied, *"we can talk while I'm washing the car."*

"I'm the one who stole your property," he explained. *"You can call the police! I don't know why I did it. You had so many beautiful things, that I didn't have!"*

I stood there in astonishment and disbelief! This man had been a life long friend! All I could say was, *"Why?"*

He began to explain how he was tempted when he knew I was away for a few days. He told how he came after midnight, broke in the door and took our things.

I thought on the matter for a while. If I called the police, he would surely go to jail. His family would suffer disgrace.

Finally, I said, *"I forgive you, and we will never mention this matter again!"* To this day, I have never told anyone; and when this book is published, it will be the first time my wife realizes that I know the thief.

He gave me a check for $3,000.00 to cover the loss of several mechanical banks he had sold; and to cover the expenses we had incurred trying to recover our things.

Well, back to the matter at hand. We had come home from Jamaica, and were in the process of selling our furniture and personal belongings.

A number of our heirlooms and valuable pieces of furniture were given to our son and daughter.

Simultaneously, we were preparing a container of medical supplies, clothing, and food for Jamaica. I threw in a few practical pieces of furniture and articles for our new home.

Everything else was put on the auction block!

The day of the sale, it was cold and rainy. I asked the auctioneer if we should postpone the sale, but he wanted to go on with it.

I went to pick up Trudee at the little apartment we had rented. We were hoping that the auction would bring in at least $15,000.00, but due to the bad weather, I told Trudee not to expect too much. We probably wouldn't have much of a crowd.

When we drove up to the house, I was amazed at the huge crowd. All day long, the people kept coming, standing in the rain, until the last article had been sold.

When we added up the revenue from the sale, it was twice as much as we were hoping for! Thank God for his faithfulness!

Yet, this was a very traumatic day for us! All day long, we watched as articles of monetary and sentimental value were carried from our home, until at the end of the day, the house stood empty!

Unless you've walked this road, giving up almost everything for the sake of the gospel, you wouldn't understand how we felt!

In the midst of all this trauma, and tearing away from things, I received a collect phone call from Jamaica. It was O'Neil.

I accepted the charge, and the first words out of his mouth were, *"Pop, I have my half, where's yours?"*

O'Neil went on to complete the six month course with YWAM; after which he attended Christ For The Nations Institute in Montego Bay, receiving a diploma from that Institution.

In the process of time, he came to live with us; and although he is not our natural son, we have come to look upon him as such!

He has been a great blessing, helping me with the ministry; and also in helping Trudee during times that her health was failing.

After completing his training at Christ For The Nations, O'Neil became the youth leader at the church. He has been used mightily by God to touch the lives of many young people.

Sometimes, as I sit and reflect upon what God has done, I'm amazed at how God could take a man of retirement age; a man who had experienced the loss of everything; and raise him up into a ministry of helping to build and strengthen the kingdom of God!

As I observe my Jamaican son, O'Neil, and consider the lives that have been affected by his ministry, I am eternally grateful to God for using me to influence his life.

And, I understand, that in God's eyes, my life is more prominent now, than when I owned houses and lands, and commanded the respect of the business community.

When I think about the people O'Neil has brought into the kingdom of God; and those he has strengthened through his prayers, his care, and his wisdom; I'm reminded that even one of those souls is infinitely more valuable than all of the heirlooms, silver, china, crystal, antiques and paintings in the entire world!

"But indeed I also count all things loss for the excellence of the knowledge of Christ Jesus my Lord, for whom I have suffered the loss of all things, and count them as rubbish, that I may gain Christ!" (Philippians 3:8).

Chapter 19

The Infirmary

I was free! Free at last! Where I once had 2,000 acres of land; not just for the business, but also for such things as hunting and fishing; now, I had not even one square foot!

Where I once had an automobile, a four wheel drive vehicle, and my wife her own car; now, we had one small economy car, which we shipped to Jamaica.

Where we once had a large, lavishly furnished home, fully paid for by years of toil; now, we had an apartment in West Virginia and a home in Jamaica, both rented!

But, I want you to understand something; I was free! All of those constant worries and concerns about managing businesses, homes, and properties were gone! I truly had peace in my heart, and I was free to serve God!

In Jamaica, church is the main focus of Christian life. It's not like the states where Christians have all sorts of other distractions.

Four nights out of the week, we would be at the church; Sunday evening services, Bible study, youth night, choir practice, and sometimes other special services.

In addition, there were other Christian organizations that had Bible studies and prayer groups. Very quickly, I became quite busy, but also well received by the Jamaican people.

One Sunday after church, the children suggested that we go to the Infirmary and have a service. They would sing, and I would preach. At the time, I had never heard of, nor knew anything about the Infirmary. I wasn't prepared for the shock!

The people were the poorest of the poor! Many were elderly, many crippled, some were mentally or physically handicapped. To put it bluntly, it seemed to be a place where people were thrown away!

The beds were rusty, bent in the middle, and most without mattresses. There were chamber pots under the beds that contained excrement. Rubber padding where the incontinent lay were filled with urine. I could hardly enter the rooms because of the stench!

I walked over to one young man, who lay staring at the ceiling. I asked how long he had been there? He retold a story of how he had fallen out of a coconut tree and broken his back. As a result, he now was paralyzed, and needed someone to feed and clean him! Everyday, for the past four years, he had just laid there, staring up at an unpainted ceiling!

There were others that couldn't walk. Some just lay on the concrete floor; others scooted themselves along on their buttocks. You could see calluses on their hips!

One woman told me she hadn't had any water. When I inquired, I was informed that the pipeline had been turned off for several days; and even though they had a cistern, the water was unfit to drink.

The cistern was large, 32 feet across and 16 feet deep, but it was full of filth! Men and women alike were standing by the cistern; completely naked; being hosed down to clean their bodies!

There were no screens or dividers of any type in the entire place to provide privacy. Whatever was done, was done in full view of everyone else!

Some patients were obviously going to die in a short time. They just lay on the floor, receiving no care or attention, waiting for the inevitable!

I had seen many things in my life, but nothing to compare to the infirmary! I just broke down and cried!

But then, God's direction came to me! *"Bring in hospital beds, sheets, pillows, medicine, bandages!"* It suddenly dawned upon me; *"this is why I was here!"*

I had never asked anyone else for help. I had always done things myself, but here was something that was more than I could handle.

I humbled myself, and wrote letters to all the people I knew, telling them the situation, and asking for their help!

When I went back to the states, I visited churches and Christian organizations. I showed them photographs of the people, I showed them photographs of the conditions; and then I asked them, *"please help!"*

Many people caught the vision. One such man had a structural steel business; and his company operated what was called an *"Inland Port."* He would receive our supplies, pack them in containers, and ship them to Jamaica.

He was already experienced in this type of operation, having shipped containers to Africa for a team of medical doctors. This was truly a blessing, for I had no idea of the amount of work required for such an endeavor.

A man called from a church 100 miles away to say he had located 20 hospital beds. He would buy the beds and have them transported to the inland port.

A lady in the Romney area told me about hospital beds that were not being used by the local hospital. I approached the county commissioners, and they gave me the beds.

A trucker called and said he would pick up the beds from the local hospital, and any other beds that needed to be transported to the inland port.

Many other people became involved, and when it was all done, we had acquired a total of 54 hospital beds. In addition, we also had crutches, walkers, chamber chairs, bandages, sheets and much more.

It required two containers in order to pack everything we had received; and $6,000.00, which I did not have, to ship them to Jamaica.

Someone suggested that I see a certain benevolent man who was well known for his humanitarian work. He and his family had donated a burn center to the Dominican Republic. He gave me a check for $5,000.00.

Others gave donations, bringing the total to $9,000.00. Before the project was completed, we needed every penny!

Back in Jamaica, there was all sorts of coordination, and especially cooperation that was needed in order to complete this project!

I went to see a member of the Jamaican Parliament from our district. He suggested that we ship the containers through the Red Cross, so we wouldn't have to pay duty.

There was the problem of getting the containers from Kingston up to Mandeville, a distance of about 60 miles. A construction firm agreed to deliver them at a reduced rate.

There were many, many other details that had to be worked out, too many to share! And, let me also emphasize; getting things done in the islands takes considerably more time than in the states, where you just pick up the phone, and arrange things in a few hours!

It was more than two months before the containers arrived; and were subsequently released by customs officials to the local Red Cross. Eventually though, I received a phone call that the containers were on the Red Cross compound, and could be picked up.

Staying in my home at the time, were a couple of ministers visiting from the states, so they went down to Kingston with me.

When we arrived, we discovered that the customs officials had broken the seals on the containers, unloaded a large number of beds onto the concrete, and just left them there!

It was a hot, humid, tropical island day. Those ministers got a good initiation into the missions work in Jamaica as we reloaded the beds and other supplies that had been strewn about!

It was a big day when we finally got those beds and other supplies to the Infirmary. Of course, we weren't finished! We now faced the task of getting the beds into the wards, and transferring the patients into the beds!

In the following days, as I walked through the wards, I saw how the people were blessed. I felt there should be a dedication of the beds and supplies to give thanks to the Lord.

The mayor of Mandeville, and several members of the Parrish Council came to the dedication. We had prayer, scripture reading and songs by the children from the church.

After I dedicated the beds and supplies to the glory of God; a reception was given. A cake was cut, and sandwiches, punch, and ice cream were served to the guests and patients.

To this day, whenever I conduct services at the Infirmary, I bring a treat of ice cream, or sometimes a bun with cheese for the patients. It's about the only treat they ever receive!

After the dedication, I was interviewed by a reporter from the Gleaner Newspaper; the biggest paper on the island. When the story appeared in the paper a week later, it gave much credence to my ministry. I give God the glory!

I had read about a Presbyterian youth group in Tennessee called the Son Servants. Each year, they would bring 200-300 young people to Jamaica for various missions projects.

I made contact with the group, and they agreed to send a team to Mandeville. When they arrived, of course, I introduced them to the Infirmary!

These young people were full of energy and zeal. They immediately began the task of restoring the cistern. In my mind, I can still see them cleaning out all that filth.

The boys would stand on the rim of the cistern and throw buckets with ropes tied to them into the water sixteen feet below. They would haul the water to the top, and the girls would dump the buckets. It took two whole days to empty the cistern!

Afterwards, they scrubbed the entire cistern with Clorox, and then painted it!

One of the team members was an engineer. He devised a plan whereby a cover was constructed for the cistern in order to keep the dirt and filth out. Then, he added a pump to draw out the water.

Every year, this group has sent a team. They have constructed a wash room, an extra ward, and ramps for wheel chairs. I can't begin to tell you what a blessing they have been!

Yet, the greatest blessing of all, is the fact that many of the patients at the Infirmary have come to know the Lord!

Even with all the improvements that have been made, the patients still don't have much to look forward to on a daily basis! About the only thing they have to look forward to, is the fact that Jesus has gone to prepare a place for them, and will return again to receive them!

I believe it can truly be said concerning these people, *"And God will wipe away every tear from their eyes; there shall be no more death, nor sorrow, nor crying; and there shall be no more pain, for the former things have passed away."* (Revelation 21:4).

Chapter 20

Saving The Children

Most Americans see Jamaica through the eyes of the tourist industry. They see hotels, sandy beaches, sparkling seas and laughing Jamaicans playing Reggae music.

The sad truth is, Jamaica is a very poor country. There is much suffering and hunger! Unfortunately, in Jamaican culture, it's often the children who suffer the most!

If you remember, when we still lived in West Vriginia, God led us to take in a young 15 year old boy. I didn't realize it at the time, but God was already preparing me for a phase of my ministry in Jamaica.

After our Jamaican son, O'Neil Sherman finished his training at Youth With A Mission, he came to live with us. This proved to be a good arrangement. He drove the van, and in many other ways helped me with the ministry.

We were traveling back and forth to the states, and it was good to have someone staying in the house. In Jamaica, it's not wise to leave your house unattended!

During those times that we were back in the states, O'Neil would bring his younger brother, Dameon up to the house to stay with him, so he wouldn't be so lonely. Then, when we returned, I would send Dameon back to his parents.

One day when I was at the grocery store, standing in line at the check out counter, I felt a tug on my pants. There stood 10 year old Dameon in his khaki school uniform. He said, *"Pop, when can I come up to the house and live with you?"*

I thought about the location of his home. It was 15 miles from the school in Mandeville. Every morning, he had to get up at 4:00 AM, walk two miles to the main road, and then catch public transportation to Mandeville. In the evening, he had to repeat the same thing, getting home around 7:00 PM.

In Jamaica, there are no school buses. You either walk or take public transportation. It's a fact that some parents don't send their children to school, because they can't afford the cost of public transportation.

Dameon's parents gave me guardianship over him; so now, we had a new member of our household. God would provide!

O'Neil and Dameon go often to visit their parents. Their parents and I also have a good relationship. They sometimes send me honey from their bee hives as well as other produce.

There were times when we shipped in other containers, filled mostly with shoes and clothing. We would set it up in our front yard, and a work team would separate the clothes and match up the shoes.

Then, we would open our gates at 10:00 AM, and the people would be allowed to come in and take whatever they needed.

The trouble was, the people would start gathering by the gate at 4:00 in the morning! They would push and shove one another, and sometimes climb over the fence to be first! We would have to close the container door, restore order, and start over.

Some of the other missionaries were visibly shaken by this scene of desperation! The needs are definitely great in Jamaica.

Most Americans, Christians included, do not have a true concept of poverty. I remember a young, Mexican man who worked for us. He was recently divorced, and was attending the church where I was ministering.

Trudee and I could see that he desired to serve God, so we encouraged him to attend Gospel Crusade in Florida. He accepted the challenge; enrolled, and completed the course of study. His life was changed, and now he has remarried, and is ministering to his fellow Mexicans.

One of this man's friends, in his broken English, asked me one day, *"Mr. Ewers, do you know what poor is?"*

I answered, *"yes, I believe so, but what do you say poor is?"*

He said, *"poor is a ten member family living in a one room, bamboo shack; a dirt floor; no running water; no toilet; very little food; no work; and the oldest child is expected to leave so the other children will have food!"* Now, that's poor!

Unfortunately, such conditions could be duplicated over and over in Jamaica!

One time, a Jamaican woman brought a young boy to the container to see if she could find some clothes and shoes to fit him.

She had found him just wandering along the side of the road. He was dirty, and was wearing only a torn pair of shorts.

Dameon took him to the outside shower and got him cleaned up. Some missionary ladies found him a set of clothes and some shoes. When he reappeared, he looked like a different boy!

His name was Artly. He didn't know his age, nor could he read or write. He was what Jamaicans call a *"Jacket Child."* That is, one who was not fathered by the same man as his brothers and sisters.

Artly had run away from home because of mistreatment. He had been living in the open air markets, begging and scrounging for food and money.

This type of thing is not uncommon in Jamaica. Sometimes, young boys are thrust out of their homes just because they're the oldest child. The mother has to care for so many other younger children, that the oldest boy is sent out to fend for himself. I'm talking about 11 and 12 year old boys!

Artly became very attached to me, but I wasn't able to take him in, because I already had O'Neil and Dameon living with me.

I found him a good, Christian home, but he stayed only a short time before running away. In all, I placed him in about five good, Christian homes, but every time, he would run away.

I would hear a noise outside my bedroom window at night. A voice would call to me, *"Pop, it is Artly!"*

I would let him in, and he would plead with me, *"Pop, I love you! I want to live with you!"*

Unfortunately, in the last home where I placed him, he stole money, and the people had him arrested!

The police brought him to my home in handcuffs. He told them he had hidden the money in my house. Of course, we didn't find any money. I'm sure he told them that story, because he wanted me to know he was in jail.

He was sent to a reformatory, but quickly escaped; and once again, appeared outside my window.

O'Neil and I took him, screaming and kicking, back to the police station. We had no choice. We could have been charged with harboring a fugitive.

He ran away from the reformatory again, and reappeared outside my window. I finally agreed to take him in, if the police would release him into my custody. Everyone agreed, but then, he disappeared!

One Sunday, we came home from church and discovered that someone had broken into the house. A camera, $150.00 in cash, and some of O'Neil and Dameon's clothes were missing.

We knew it was Artly, because he left his dirty clothes when he changed into the clothes he had stolen.

Sometime later, he came by the house. I confronted him, and he admitted breaking into the house. I had to talk to him outside. He wouldn't come inside the house, because he was afraid I would call the police.

He promised to come back the next day, and return the camera. I have not seen, nor heard from him since!

Artly's story could be duplicated over and over throughout Jamaica. There are thousands of young boys running loose, trying to survive. Most of them end up in trouble!

I came home about noon one day, and again, discovered that someone had broken into my house. I had quite a substantial loss, so I called the police. They came a day later, which is not unusual, and took fingerprints.

Two days later, the police asked me to come to the station and identify some of my things they had recovered. They had charged a 15 year old boy with the burglary.

Two big officers picked up this young boy by the seat of his pants, threw him in a chair, and started slapping him to get a confession.

I tried to get them to stop the beating, but I was ordered not to interfere.

They proceeded to use a whip with seven or eight, long, leather straps to get a confession. The boy fell from the chair and covered his face with his hands and arms. He gave them whatever confession they wanted!

Afterwards, they threw him back into a dungeon like cell.

His confession led the police to two other young brothers where he had taken the stolen things. After about two days of questioning, it was determined that the two brothers thought the 15 year old boy had received the stolen things from a cousin in the states.

During this time, I was asking the Lord what I should do? I ended up ministering to the two brothers, one in his early twenties, and the other age 11.

The 11 year old, whose name was Steve, had been abandoned by his mother two years earlier. After wandering around on his own for a year, his older brother had found him, and was trying to take care of him.

This is where I entered the picture. Steve had absolutely nothing. He was uneducated, and couldn't even read or write his name. He spoke only the local Jamaican dialect, called *"Patois,"* also known as Jamaican Creole.

So, I took him into my home. Now, I had three boys! Praise the Lord! He provides for all our needs!

Steve is now attending school, learning the basics of education. He can do things like write his name, and tell time, which he could not do when he first came to live with me!

He's a good, young boy. He has accepted the Lord, and has been baptized!

I am now his only family. If he were to die, I would just have to bury him. There is no one to contact!

I have often thought about starting an orphanage. If I had 1,000 beds, they would probably be filled in a week. That would be the easy part. Finding the funds and workers to run the orphanage would be the challenge! All I can say is, *"may God's will be done!"* He has my allegiance until the day I die!

Chapter 21

"Out of Many, One People"

Although Jamaicans are predominately of African descent; there are minorities of British, Chinese, Indians, Germans, Portuguese, and those who have immigrated from other islands in the West Indies.

Many of these people have intermarried to create the population of Jamaica. Thus, that nation has adopted the motto: *"Out of Many, One People!"*

When a person goes to a foreign country as a missionary, there is one thing they must do, if they truly want to be effective. Learn to become ONE with the people!

Once every year, the Jamaican Evangelistic Association holds a big convention in Kingston. I always go, and we generally take a van full of people from Mandeville. Many people stay the entire week, sleeping on benches, or wherever they can find a place.

At the conclusion of the convention, they have a water baptism service.

Pertaining to baptism, I had never been immersed, only sprinkled as an infant. The first year I attended this convention, the Lord spoke to me to be baptized.

So, on the night of the baptism, I walked forward at the age of 65, with twenty other young Jamaicans. I was the only white person in that entire congregation of more than 800 people.

The Lord knew what he was doing. That baptism cemented me to the people of the church. I was a part of them!

The phone rang, Sister Brown was on the line. *"Brother Ewers, the owner is going to sell the church property. What are we going to do?"*

Immediately, the Holy Spirit spoke to me. *"Tell the owner you will meet with him, and work out an arrangement. That property must not revert back into a bar and dance hall!"*

The owner told us a man from England wanted to buy the property and operate it as a bar; but he offered the property to us first!

I thought for a moment, and then replied, *"I'll be going to the states soon, and I'll try to raise the money. If I give you $2,000.00 in U.S. dollars now, will you hold the property until I return?"* I told him if I failed to raise the money, he could keep the $2,000.00. We had a deal!

I had never been involved in this specific type of fund raising activity; but I had watched God perform miracles when we shipped the containers to Jamaica. The things we needed for the Infirmary were so abundantly supplied that we needed two containers!

Another time, after a hurricane had struck the island, I had seen God take $2,000.00 and purchase $10,000.00 worth of flour to send to the people.

God is a great God, and I knew he was well able to provide the additional funds we needed to purchase the property.

I was gone for three weeks, speaking in churches, and talking to everybody I knew. When I returned, I had $16,000.00.

I was praising God and thanking him for his faithfulness. Sister Brown was praising God too, but I could see a worried look on her face!

While I was gone, there was a misunderstanding in the church. Most of the people had left! That next Sunday, there was Sister Brown, myself and three others in church!

This type of thing is common in Jamaica, but to me, it was new, and serious!

I told her it was a good thing that I didn't know the situation. I might not have tried to raise the funds.

She calmly told me, *"Brother Ewers, the battle is the Lord's, and we'll just continue to pray and be faithful!"*

One evening, the telephone rang. A first cousin that I had not heard from for years was calling from Nevada. He had heard about my work in Jamaica, and wanted to send a contribution.

He said he loved the Lord; but wondered if I would have a problem accepting a donation from a registered gambler?

I had heard that he had been quite successful! I told him to send whatever God put upon his heart. Wherever the money comes from, I'll put it to work for God!

The donation was enough to complete the purchase of the church property, as well as another building on the property, which was developed into Sunday school rooms, and a sewing center. I'll say more about the sewing center in a few paragraphs.

In all, more than $40,000.00 was raised or given to help the church. We chartered the church after the name of the local community: *"Royal Flat Community Faith Church."* Sister Brown and I were appointed as overseers; O'Neil was appointed as the youth leader, and once again, the church began to grow!

One day, the Lord spoke to me about starting a sewing center in the church. We had this extra building on the property; and there was a shirt manufacturing factory within a mile from the church.

I talked with the management of the shirt factory to see if we could train some workers, and get some contract work. Maybe we could provide employment for some of the ladies in the church.

On my next trip to the states, the Lord provided funds for six commercial type sewing machines. After some hard work electrically wiring the building, our sewing center is now in operation; but not as I had envisioned!

The management at the shirt factory had changed, and I was not able to work out an agreement with the new management.

However, I was able to make a contract with a local coffee company to sew burlap bags in which they market coffee to tourists. We now sew about 4,000 bags a week.

First, 10% of the gross income is given as a tithe to the church. Then, we've been able to provide employment for some of the ladies in the church; we have established a school lunch program for the children; and additional funds are used to help the poor!

Sometimes, people have the idea that missionary work consists only of preaching the gospel and casting out devils; but many times, it's just helping people in the name of the Lord.

I met a young minister from a small town called May Pen, which is about 30 miles from Mandeville.

He and his wife had attended Christ For The Nations with O'Neil; and they were now having church services in a small tent located in a cow pasture.

I felt led of the Lord to begin helping this church. Now, one Sunday a month, I travel to May Pen for their church services. Whenever I have clothes, treats, or other goods, I share them with the people of this church.

I've established a good relationship with this pastor and his wife; and with God's help, we're someday going to acquire a piece of land, and build a permanent church!

Primarily, I've been called to minister to the poor and needy of this beautiful island nation; but once in a while, the Lord puts you in the company of royalty.

On one visit to Kingston, I was invited to dinner by the secretary of the Prime Minister. It was an excellent affair; the ladies in long, fancy dresses; and everything done in a most proper manner.

One man who attended this dinner was a minister. I didn't realize he was the overseer of one of the largest denominations on the island. He asked me to speak at a particular church function. I accepted, thinking that I would be speaking to a small group of people.

When I arrived, we entered an outside arena which seated over 2,000; and it was full! All I could say was, *"Lord, help!"* And, God did help me! I was invited to minister the next night!

This in turn, opened doors for meeting other prominent Jamaican Christians. One such Christian layman lived in as fine a house as I have ever seen. Through his initial influence, came the formation of a FGBMFI chapter in Kingston.

At one of the FGBMFI planning meetings, a Colonel in the Jamaican Army attended. He was a big, tall man; well respected wherever he went. I can still hear him coming down the hallway, loudly declaring, *"Praise the Lord!"*

I stayed at this Colonel's home the night before our charter meeting. Also staying at his home was the Supreme Court Justice of the island nation of Grenada. He was to be the speaker at the meeting.

That initial meeting was quite an event. It was attended by representatives from other Caribbean island nations, the United States, and 300 or more Jamaicans.

The morning after the meeting, we held an impromptu prayer meeting in the lobby of the hotel. A message in tongues and interpretation came forth, *"Jamaica was to be the center of a tremendous revival, which would affect all the Caribbean; and the Lord was now positioning his men and women for this move of God!"*

I believe this was truly a word from the Lord; and I am pleased to say that I am now a part of this revival!

And this revival is not in word only, but in demonstration and power of the Holy Spirit. I'm reminded of the simple story of a 12 year old, Jamaican girl, whose mother had breast cancer.

The night before the mother was to leave for Kingston to have an operation, the little girl pulled an empty chair up beside her bed.

She took her mother's hand, and began to pray, *"Jesus, I want you to come sit in this chair! Jesus, if your mother was sick, and I could heal her; and you asked me to do it, I would! So, I ask you to heal my mother. I need her very badly! If she would die, I would have nowhere to go. You are the only person I know that can make her well. Jesus, will you please heal my mother?"*

The following morning, when the mother awoke, she was lying on her breast. Previously, she could not do so because of the pain! She examined her breast and discovered that there was no seepage.

When the doctor in Kingston examined her, he could find no trace of the cancer. All the X-rays and tests were negative!

We serve a great God! There is nothing too difficult for him! In the coming years, as long as the Lord gives me breath, I expect to see more of his mighty power and grace!

Chapter 22

And The Work Goes On!

I came with three suitcases! No church or individual sent me out. I came by faith! I sold my home, and my personal belongings. The only income I had was my social security.

Now, as I stand on the veranda of my rented Jamaican home, looking out over the mountains and the valleys below, I give thanks to God! He has given me back much more than I left behind! You see, I have found a peace that I never thought was possible!

I have a purpose for my life that causes me to continually experience Psalm 103:5, *"....your youth is renewed like the eagle's!"*

Sometimes when I return to the states, I have the opportunity to observe older, retired people. More often than not, their talents, their experience; and sadly, the remaining years of their lives are being wasted!

It seems that many older, retired people are just routinely going about their daily lives, pursuing nothing but trivial and meaningless goals; and waiting for death!

The fact is, older Christians of retirement age have much to offer for the service of God! They have the time; and most of them also have the financial resources!

Some older people claim they can't do much for God because of their health. I want you to know that God has made provision! Psalm 103, verses 2-3 says: *"Bless the Lord, O my soul; and forget not all His benefits: who forgives all your iniquities, WHO HEALS ALL YOUR DISEASES!"*

Many times, God has restored my health. Once, my breathing had become difficult. I was taking oxygen, and couldn't walk up hills. I asked God to heal me; and now, I walk over a mile each day, up and down hills!

Another time, I had a slipped disk in my back. I was sent home and put into traction. Again, I asked God to heal me so I could continue his work. Now, I'm able to move freely about with no problem!

I developed an allergy, and asked God to heal me. Now, I breathe freely, and my eyes are not swollen! God is faithful to his Word!

Trudee's health has deteriorated over the years. She's no longer able to stand by my side in ministry.

It saddened me when I had to leave her in West Virginia, and return to Jamaica to serve God alone. She has released me to fulfill my ministry, and that I shall do!

But, I'm not really alone! God has told me in his word, *"....I will never leave you nor forsake you."* (Hebrews 13:5). Besides that, God has also given me the companionship of a Jamaican family!

Yet, there is no doubt in my heart, nor questions in my mind, that the Lord's benefit of healing is also available to Trudee! God is not only able, but willing to raise her up, and restore her health and strength! I pray that she will truly trust God in this matter!

God's not finished with me yet! I'm 71 years old at the publication of this book, and I look forward to serving God many more years.

The Lord impressed upon me to establish a ministry that would be above reproach; one which would demonstrate accountability here in Jamaica!

I've seen too much abuse of funds given for the Lord's work in Jamaica. During any given week, Jamaican ministers are boarding airplanes for the United States; working their way up and down the East Coast, preaching and raising money for their church.

After five or six months in the states, they return with thousands of dollars. All to often, the minister's personal desires take priority over the needs of the church, so the money never goes where it was intended!

The ministry I've established, *"Servant's Heart Ministry,"* will not be so! It will be a ministry of integrity!

It is duly registered in Jamaica; and has an excellent Jamaican board of directors, who oversee the distribution of every dollar. And, let me emphasize that every dollar donated goes 100% to God's work here in Jamaica.

I didn't ask for all this ministry. I only wanted to come and help; but God keeps imparting a vision to build and expand! As I was nearing completion of this book, *"Servant's Heart Ministry"* was able to purchase a seven bedroom house on 4/10 of an acre in downtown Mandeville.

On this property, we plan to establish a church, a bakery, and a trade center. The house can be used for visiting missionaries; and we are praying about a home for street children.

Please pray with me that every financial need will be met, that we might move forward with the vision! With God's help, and for his glory, it shall be fulfilled!

The End

A Prayer To Receive Christ

Are you a Christian? Has there been a time in your life, when you can truly say that you accepted Jesus Christ into your life?

A great many Jamaicans believe they are Christians, because their mother taught them the Bible, or because they've been in church all their lives.

But, there must be a time, when you, and you alone, personally invite Jesus Christ into your life! Has there been such a time in your life? If not, I invite you to pray with me right now!

"Heavenly Father, I come to you in the name of Jesus Christ.

Thank you for sending Jesus to die on the cross for my sins. The Bible says his shed blood is able to cleanse me from all sin, and give me a right standing before God.

Heavenly Father, I believe you raised Jesus Christ from the dead. He is alive now, and he can come to dwell in my heart by his Spirit.

Lord Jesus, at this moment, I personally invite you into my life to be my Savior and my God!

Cleanse me with the blood you shed upon the cross. Make me clean, and give me a right standing before my Heavenly Father!

Thank you for coming into my heart. According to your word, I am now born again!

And, from this moment forward, I declare that you, Lord Jesus, are my Lord and my God!"

AMEN

Randolph L. Ewers
can be contacted at;

and....

Additional copies of this book
can be ordered from:

Servant's Heart Ministry
P. O. Box 654
Mandeville, Manchester
Jamaica, West Indies

All proceeds from the sale
of this book, go 100% for
the Lord's work in Jamaica!

Notes